Oxford Introductions to Language Study

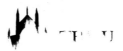

Phonetics

Peter Roach is Emeritus Professor of
Phonetics at the University of Reading

D1643347

Oxford Introductions to Language Study

Series Editor H.G.Widdowson

Phonetics

Peter Roach

OXFORD
UNIVERSITY PRESS

OXFORD
UNIVERSITY PRESS

Great Clarendon Street, Oxford OX2 6DP

Oxford University Press is a department of the University of Oxford.
It furthers the University's objective of excellence in research, scholarship,
and education by publishing worldwide in

Oxford New York

Auckland Cape Town Dar es Salaam Hong Kong Karachi
Kuala Lumpur Madrid Melbourne Mexico City Nairobi
New Delhi Shanghai Taipei Toronto

With offices in

Argentina Austria Brazil Chile Czech Republic France Greece
Guatemala Hungary Italy Japan Poland Portugal Singapore
South Korea Switzerland Thailand Turkey Ukraine Vietnam

OXFORD and OXFORD ENGLISH are registered trade marks of
Oxford University Press in the UK and in certain other countries

ISBN-13: 978 0 19 437239 8

Typeset by G.M. Brasnett, Cambridge
in Adobe Sabon & ITC Franklin Gothic

Printed in China

Contents

Preface

Purpose

What justification might there be for a series of introductions to language study? After all, linguistics is already well served with introductory texts: expositions and explanations which are comprehensive, authoritative, and excellent in their way. Generally speaking, however, their way is the essentially academic one of providing a detailed initiation into the discipline of linguistics, and they tend to be lengthy and technical: appropriately so, given their purpose. But they can be quite daunting to the novice. There is also a need for a more general and gradual introduction to language: transitional texts which will ease people into an understanding of complex ideas. This series of introductions is designed to serve this need.

Their purpose, therefore, is not to supplant but to support the more academically oriented introductions to linguistics: to prepare the conceptual ground. They are based on the belief that it is an advantage to have a broad map of the terrain sketched out before one considers its more specific features on a smaller scale, a general context in reference to which the detail makes sense. It is sometimes the case that students are introduced to detail without it being made clear what it is a detail *of*. Clearly, a general understanding of ideas is not sufficient: there needs to be closer scrutiny. But equally, close scrutiny can be myopic and meaningless unless it is related to the larger view. Indeed, it can be said that the precondition of more particular enquiry is an awareness of what, in general, the particulars are about. This series is designed to provide this large-scale view of different areas of language study. As such it can serve as a preliminary to (and precondition for) the more specific and specialized enquiry which students of linguistics are required to undertake.

But the series is not only intended to be helpful to such students. There are many people who take an interest in language without being academically engaged in linguistics *per se*. Such people may recognize the importance of understanding language for their own lines of enquiry, or for their own practical purposes, or quite simply for making them aware of something which figures so centrally in their everyday lives. If linguistics has revealing and relevant things to say about language, this should presumably not be a privileged revelation, but one accessible to people other than linguists. These books have been so designed as to accommodate these broader interests too: they are meant to be introductions to language more generally as well as to linguistics as a discipline.

Design

The books in the series are all cut to the same basic pattern. There are four parts: Survey, Readings, References, and Glossary.

Survey

This is a summary overview of the main features of the area of language study concerned: its scope and principles of enquiry, its basic concerns and key concepts. These are expressed and explained in ways which are intended to make them as accessible as possible to people who have no prior knowledge or expertise in the subject. The Survey is written to be readable and is uncluttered by the customary scholarly references. In this sense, it is simple. But it is not simplistic. Lack of specialist expertise does not imply an inability to understand or evaluate ideas. Ignorance means lack of knowledge, not lack of intelligence. The Survey, therefore, is meant to be challenging. It draws a map of the subject area in such a way as to stimulate thought and to invite a critical participation in the exploration of ideas. This kind of conceptual cartography has its dangers of course: the selection of what is significant, and the manner of its representation, will not be to the liking of everybody, particularly not, perhaps, to some of those inside the discipline. But these surveys are written in the belief that there must be an alternative to a technical account on the one hand and an idiot's guide on the other if linguistics is to be made relevant to people in the wider world.

Readings

Some people will be content to read, and perhaps re-read, the summary Survey. Others will want to pursue the subject and so will use the Survey as the preliminary for more detailed study. The Readings provide the necessary transition. For here the reader is presented with texts extracted from the specialist literature. The purpose of these Readings is quite different from the Survey. It is to get readers to focus on the specifics of what is said, and how it is said, in these source texts. Questions are provided to further this purpose: they are designed to direct attention to points in each text, how they compare across texts, and how they deal with the issues discussed in the Survey. The idea is to give readers an initial familiarity with the more specialist idiom of the linguistics literature, where the issues might not be so readily accessible, and to encourage them into close critical reading.

References

One way of moving into more detailed study is through the Readings. Another is through the annotated References in the third section of each book. Here there is a selection of works (books and articles) for further reading. Accompanying comments indicate how these deal in more detail with the issues discussed in the different chapters of the Survey.

Glossary

Certain terms in the Survey appear in bold. These are terms used in a special or technical sense in the discipline. Their meanings are made clear in the discussion, but they are also explained in the Glossary at the end of each book. The Glossary is cross-referenced to the Survey, and therefore serves at the same time as an index. This enables readers to locate the term and what it signifies in the more general discussion, thereby, in effect, using the Survey as a summary work of reference.

Use

The series has been designed so as to be flexible in use. Each title is separate and self-contained, with only the basic format in common. The four sections of the format, as described here, can be drawn upon and combined in different ways, as required by the needs, or interests, of different readers. Some may be content with the Survey and the Glossary and may not want to follow up the suggested References. Some may not wish to venture into the Readings. Again, the Survey might be considered as appropriate preliminary reading for a course in applied linguistics or teacher education, and the Readings more appropriate for seminar discussion during the course. In short, the notion of an introduction will mean different things to different people, but in all cases the concern is to provide access to specialist knowledge and stimulate an awareness of its significance. This series as a whole has been designed to provide this access and promote this awareness in respect to different areas of language study.

H.G. WIDDOWSON

1

The science of speech

Speaking to each other is one of the most interesting things that we human beings do. Each of us has a mind, a private world filled with thoughts, feelings, and memories. We have many ways of communicating these in such a way that they enter the minds of other people. Sometimes we find it convenient to communicate by means of writing, and good writing can let us see things clearly from the writer's own perspective. For people who are for some reason unable to speak, it is also possible to communicate by sign language, or by using a pointer and a computer screen. Many art-forms work by conveying the thoughts and feelings of the artist— music, for example, can tell us a great deal about the inner feelings of a composer, even one who has been dead for centuries.

A quite different form of communication is one that we share with many other animals: gestures and facial expressions. We make extensive use of these, and can describe in great detail how people do so: we can talk about someone 'waving his hand dismissively', or 'giving someone an appealing look', or 'turning away in mock anger'. But although there are many different ways of communicating, when it comes to telling other people what we want to tell them, what we use most is speech, and this is something which is only available to human beings.

The speech chain

To describe the process of speaking in the simplest way, we need to look at three main events. To begin with, we produce sounds, using parts of our chest, throat, and head. Then the sounds travel through the air in the form of vibrations. Finally, the sounds are

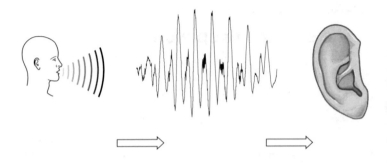

FIGURE 1.1 *The speech chain*

received by the ear of the listener. We show this speech chain in diagram form in Figure 1.1.

However, this is only part of the story. If we look at speech more carefully, we find we must also take into account the fact that the brain of the speaker is involved in controlling the production of speech, and the brain of the listener has to do the job of analysing the sounds that have been heard, and converting them into a meaningful message. You might say of someone, in a joking way, that they were speaking without first connecting their brain, or that what was said to them went 'in one ear and out of the other', but in reality the control by the brain is essential. Not only does the brain send out the commands necessary for producing speech, but it is also constantly receiving feedback in the form of the sound of the speech that is being produced; if we were not able to monitor our speaking in this way, we would find it extremely difficult to speak at all. Until recently, we knew little about what is going on in the brain when people are speaking, and this is why the science of phonetics has concentrated on the three central components of the speech chain, where observation of what is going on is relatively straightforward. However, our understanding of how the brain works in speech communication has grown enormously in recent years. One of the most significant advances in recent research has been the development of safe and accurate brain-scanning techniques that can show us the activity of different parts of the brain when someone is speaking or listening to speech.

Phonetics

Speech is a complicated process, and to study it requires a whole scientific subject—the science of phonetics. In this book we will look at the main areas of phonetics and see why they are important. Much of the early part of the book is taken up with considering the way in which speech sounds (often called **segments**) are made, and how phoneticians can classify them in a scientific way. This is based on the fundamental distinction between **vowels** and **consonants**. Another fundamental aspect of the subject is the use of symbols. In phonetics, we must be able to use a particular symbol to represent a particular sound. This is quite similar to the principle of alphabetic writing: some writing systems give a very clear indication of the sounds (for example, the writing systems of Finnish and Italian represent almost perfectly the sequence of sounds required to say something in those languages). At the other extreme, it is possible to have what we call an *ideographic* writing system where symbols represent ideas, not sounds. The nearest equivalent for users of alphabetic writing is our number system: the numbers 1, 2, 3 mean the same thing to speakers of Russian, of French, or of English, yet they would pronounce them in completely different ways.

One of the most important achievements of phonetics in the past century has been to arrive at a system of phonetic symbols that anyone can learn to use and that can be used to represent the sounds of any language. This is the **International Phonetic Alphabet (IPA)**. Taking English as an example of a writing system that does not always give a reliable guide to pronunciation, we find that for various purposes (including teaching the pronunciation) it is helpful to use **phonetic transcription** instead of ordinary spelling. Many of the symbols we use are the same as the familiar alphabetic ones. Table 1.1 shows the symbols used to represent one accent of English, and the symbols are given with 'key words' which help you to see which sound is represented. For each of the many different **accents** of English, a slightly different set of symbols might be needed. The 'standard accent' of English described in this book is similar to one which for much of the twentieth century was known by the name **Received Pronunciation** (**RP** for short); an increasing number of modern writers on phonetics (including some whose works appear in the Readings and References sections of this book) now prefer to use the name **BBC accent**, and that is what is done here. I am not, of course, claiming that all speakers on the BBC have the same accent, and an increasing number of professional broadcasters now have Irish, Scottish, or Welsh accents, but it is still possible to identify a reasonably consistent pronunciation used by English-born announcers and newsreaders on channels such as Radio 3 and Radio 4, BBC television news and the World Service of

---

Vowels

ɪ bit   e bet   æ bat   ʌ cut   ɒ cot   ʊ put
ə about, China

iː eat   ɑː palm   ɜː earn   ɔː paw   uː too

eɪ day   aɪ die   ɔɪ boy   aʊ how   əʊ go   ɪə fear
eə air   ʊə poor

The symbols /i/ and /u/ are also used, for weak versions of /iː/ and /uː/, as in the last vowel of 'happy' /hæpi/, or the first vowel of 'whoever' /huevə/.

Consonants

p pin   t tin   k kin   b bin   d din   g girl

f fin   θ thing   s sing   v van   ð this
ʃ shoe   h how   z zoo   ʒ measure
tʃ chin   dʒ gin

m more   n no   ŋ sing

l low   r red   w wet   j yet

TABLE 1.1 *IPA symbols used to represent the 'BBC accent' of English or 'Received Pronunciation' (RP)*

the BBC. One advantage of this choice is that anyone with a radio can listen to BBC broadcasts as much as they like; tracking down the elusive RP speaker has always been a problem for researchers, since nobody could ever agree on exactly what they should be looking for.

Using these symbols, we can write English in a way that tells you exactly which sounds are pronounced: notice how different this looks from ordinary English spelling in the example sentence:

Spelling: She bought some chairs and a table
Transcription: ʃi   bɔːt   səm   tʃeəz   ən   ə teɪbl

The symbols listed above for English represent the distinctive sounds of the language that we call **phonemes**. They are therefore a special kind of phonetic symbol that we call **phonemic** symbols. There is a technical matter concerning the use of symbols that needs to be explained here, since symbols appear through the rest of the book. When the symbols we use are those representing the phonemes of a particular language, it is usual to enclose them in 'slant brackets' (for example, 'book' is transcribed /bʊk/). When we use phonetic symbols to represent a sound that could belong to any language, or a sound which is a special way of pronouncing a phoneme (**allophone**) we enclose them in square brackets (for example, we can say that [y], [o], [u], and [ø] are all vowels made with the lips rounded).

Phonetics has links with many other subjects: when we look at the parts of the body which are used in speaking, we make use of information from anatomy and physiology; the study of the transmission of speech sounds from speaker to hearer is related to **acoustics**, which is a branch of physics; when we look at how we hear and understand spoken messages, we are in the territory of other subjects including audiology (the study of the hearing mechanism) and cognitive psychology (the study of how the brain receives and processes information).

Phonetics and linguistics

Finally, we should not forget that the whole science of phonetics is an essential part of the subject of linguistics. When we look at the subject from this point of view, we need to understand the

Consonants

	Bilabial	Labiodental	Dental	Alveolar	Post alveolar	Retroflex	Palatal	Velar	Uvular	Pharyngeal	Glottal
Plosive	p b			t d		ʈ ɖ	c ɟ	k ɡ	q ɢ		ʔ
Nasal	m	ɱ		n		ɳ	ɲ	ŋ	ɴ		
Trill	ʙ			r					ʀ		
Tap or flap		ⱱ		ɾ		ɽ					
Fricative	ɸ β	f v	θ ð	s z	ʃ ʒ	ʂ ʐ	ç ʝ	x ɣ	χ ʁ	ħ ʕ	h ɦ
Lateral Fricative				ɬ ɮ							
Approximant		ʋ		ɹ		ɻ	j	ɰ			
Lateral approximant				l		ɭ	ʎ	ʟ			

Where symbols appear in pairs, the one to the right represents a voiced consonant. Shaded areas denote articulations judged impossible.

Consonants (non-pulmonic)

Clicks		Voiced implosives		Ejectives	
ʘ	Bilabial	ɓ	Bilabial	ʼ	Examples:
ǀ	Dental	ɗ	Dental/alveolar	pʼ	Bilabial
ǃ	(Post)alveolar	ʄ	Palatal	tʼ	Dental/alveolar
ǂ	Palatoalveolar	ɠ	Velar	kʼ	Velar
ǁ	Alveolar lateral	ʛ	Uvular	sʼ	Alveolar fricative

Vowels

Where symbols appear in pairs, the one to the right represents a rounded vowel.

	Front	Central	Back
Close	i y	ɨ ʉ	ɯ u
		ɪ ʏ	ʊ	
Close-mid	e ø	ɘ ɵ	ɤ o
		ə	
Open-mid	ɛ œ	ɜ ɞ	ʌ ɔ
	æ	ɐ	
Open	a ɶ		ɑ ɒ

Other symbols

ʍ	Voiceless labial-velar fricative	ɕ ʑ	Alveolar-palatal fricatives
w	Voiced labial-velar approximant	ɺ	Alveolar lateral flap
ɥ	Voiced labial-palatal approximant	ɧ	Simultaneous ʃ and x
ʜ	Voiceless epiglottal fricative		
ʢ	Voiced epiglottal fricative	Affricates and double articulations can be represented by two symbols joined by a tie bar if necessary. k͡p t͡s	
ʡ	Epiglottal plosive		

Diacritics Diacritics may be placed above a symbol with a descender, e.g. ŋ̊

̥	Voiceless	n̥ d̥	̤ Breathy voiced	b̤ a̤	̪ Dental	t̪ d̪	
̬	Voiced	s̬ t̬	̰ Creaky voiced	b̰ a̰	̺ Apical	t̺ d̺	
ʰ	Aspirated	tʰ dʰ	̼ Linguolabial	t̼ d̼	̻ Laminal	t̻ d̻	
̹	More rounded	ɔ̹	ʷ Labialized	tʷ dʷ	̃ Nasalized	ẽ	
̜	Less rounded	ɔ̜	ʲ Palatalized	tʲ dʲ	ⁿ Nasal release	dⁿ	
̟	Advanced	u̟	ˠ Velarized	tˠ dˠ	ˡ Lateral release	dˡ	
̠	Retracted	e̠	ˤ Pharyngealized	tˤ dˤ	̚ No audible release	d̚	
̈	Centralized	ë	̴ Velarized or pharyngealized	ɫ			
̽	Mid-centralized	e̽	̝ Raised	e̝	(ɹ̝ = voiced alveolar fricative)		
̩	Syllabic	n̩	̞ Lowered	e̞	(β̞ = voiced bilabial approximant)		
̯	Non-syllabic	e̯	̘ Advanced Tongue Root	e̘			
˞	Rhoticity	ɚ a˞	̙ Retracted Tongue Root	e̙			

Suprasegmentals

ˈ	Primary stress	
ˌ	Secondary stress	ˌfoʊnəˈtɪʃən
ː	Long	eː
ˑ	Half-long	eˑ
̆	Extra-short	ĕ
ǀ	Minor (foot) group	
‖	Major (intonation) group	
.	Syllable break	ɹi.ækt
‿	Linking (absence of a break)	

Tones and word accents

Level			Contour		
e̋ or ˥	Extra high		ě or ∧	Rising	
é	˦	High	ê	∨	Falling
ē	˧	Mid	e᷄	↑	High rising
è	˨	Low	e᷅	↓	Low rise
ȅ	˩	Extra low	e᷈	↑	Rising-falling
↓	Downstep		↗	Global rise	
↑	Upstep		↘	Global fall	

TABLE 1.2 *Chart of the International Phonetic Alphabet (revised 1993, updated 1996)*

basic principle of contrast in language: in phonetics in general, we can identify an enormous variety of different sounds that humans can make, but only a small number of these are used in a particular language to make a difference between words. In French the words 'tout' (which we write in phonemic symbols as /tu/) and 'tu' (phonemically /ty/) are recognizably different because of their vowels. In English the word 'two' is phonetically [tu]; if we were to substitute the vowel [y], this would not result in an English listener hearing a different English word. This is because the set of distinctive sounds (**phonemes**), is different in French and English. The phonemes of 'BBC accent' English are listed in Table 1.1.

Linguistics studies all aspects of human language. In some cases (syntax, for example) it deals with complex and abstract concepts, and the mental processes involved can only be guessed at, not observed or measured. In other areas of linguistics, such as the study of social or regional variation in language, the data and their patterns may be easier to grasp. But, unless we are studying written language, it is only through analysing spoken language that we are able to collect the data we use in linguistic research. The great British scholar Henry Sweet described phonetics as 'the indispensable foundation' for the study of language, and that view is as valid today as it was a hundred years ago.

2

Making speech sounds

Speech and breathing

In the languages of the world there is a huge and fascinating variety of different speech sounds, and we need to understand how these speech sounds are made. The most basic fact to remember is that all the sounds we use in speech are produced by moving air. Speech is sometimes described as 'modified breathing': the process of speaking begins, except for a relatively small number of cases, with the air inside the speaker's chest escaping from the lungs, through the throat and the mouth, and out into the open air, as you can see in Figure 2.1. If we produce this flow of air without impeding it in any way, the activity would just be what we call 'breathing out', or, if we do it loudly enough to make a sound, a 'sigh' (which can convey many different meanings). But usually in speaking we use our **articulators** to modify the flow of air so that sounds are produced. When we do this, we produce a sequence of vowels and consonants that make up **syllables**: if you say 'Cut it out', for example, you are alternately obstructing the flow of air from the lungs (when you produce the consonants) and then allowing the air to escape rather easily (in the vowels). In this example, three syllables are produced. Syllables usually contain a vowel, and may start and end with one or more consonants.

It is a very interesting fact about speech that it has evolved by making use of parts of the body which already have some bio-logical reason for being there, and as far as we know there is nothing in the human body which exists exclusively for mak-ing or recognizing speech sounds. We would still need our lungs, our tongues, our vocal folds, and our ears, even if they were not required for speech.

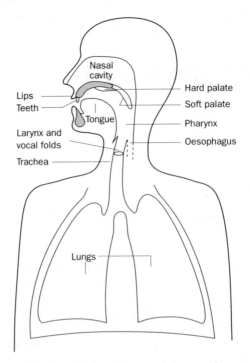

Lips
Teeth
Larynx and vocal folds
Trachea

Nasal cavity
Tongue

Hard palate
Soft palate
Pharynx
Oesophagus

Lungs

FIGURE 2.1 *The breathing system and the vocal tract*

There are, in fact, some speech sounds which are made by using something other than the lungs to make the air move. To English speakers, many of these sounds are familiar but 'non-linguistic'—they are not used as phonemes of the language: for example 'click' sounds are found when we make the 'annoyance' noise that used to be written as 'tut-tut' (or nowadays more usually as 'tsk-tsk'), and people still sometimes use a 'gee-up' click to tell a horse to move on. But in a number of languages of southern Africa such as Zulu and Xhosa, we find a wide variety of click sounds being used as consonant phonemes of the language. There are also sounds known as 'ejectives' and 'implosives' in many of the world's languages, and to produce these you have to use the larynx: the vocal folds are closed or nearly closed, and the larynx is moved upwards (in ejectives) to push air out, or downwards (in implosives) to suck air in. These sounds are found in many different languages, including some accents of English. Amharic (spoken in Ethiopia) is a good example of a language with ejective sounds, having contrasting pairs of phonemes /t/ and /t'/. The latter is ejective: the way ejectives are produced is a little like the mechanism used for spitting some small object (e.g. a grape pip) from your mouth. An example of a language with implosives is Sindhi (spoken in India). This has a /ɓ/ similar to that of English and a different phoneme /ɓ/ in which air is 'gulped' inwards by a movement of the larynx.

The passageway through which air passes from the larynx, past the lips, and out into the air outside our bodies is called the **vocal tract**. Below this is the **trachea**, the 'windpipe' which is connected to the lungs and which passes from the chest into the neck. We do not have the ability to move or modify this.

The larynx

The **larynx**, indicated in Figure 2.1, is very important. The vital part of the larynx is a pair of folds of muscular tissue called the **vocal folds**, and we can move these into a number of positions between wide open and tightly closed. We open them widely to allow a rapid escape of air. If they are slightly narrowed, so that the gap between them is only a few millimetres, the air makes a rushing noise that we associate with the sound at the beginning of the English word 'head'. If we close them enough for them to be lightly touching each other, the air passing between them causes them to vibrate; this is called **voicing**, or **phonation**, and it can be varied in many ways, most importantly in **pitch**, which may be high or low according to how we adjust our vocal folds. Many speech sounds are **voiced**, while others are **voiceless**. If you want to practise detecting the difference, compare [s] and [z]: the consonant [s] is voiceless and the only sound it makes is the hissing sound as air escapes over the tongue. However, its voiced counterpart [z] not only has this hissing sound, but also the buzzing of the vocal folds vibrating. You can hear this best if you put your fingers in your ears and produce a long, buzzing [z]. You can also detect the vibration if you press your fingers gently against your larynx as you produce the [z]. Vowels are almost always voiced, as are **nasal** consonants like [m] and [n]. Finally, if we close the vocal folds firmly, we prevent air from escaping. This is often called a **glottal stop**.

The vocal tract above the larynx

Immediately above the larynx is a passageway called the **pharynx**. This carries air, but also food when we are eating. As we all occasionally find when we are trying to eat and speak at the same time, this passageway can get rather crowded. Although we are able to narrow it if we want to, and this ability is used in some languages, its role in speech is generally small. Above the pharynx, the vocal tract divides. One passageway goes up into the nasal cavity from which air escapes through the nose; however, this only happens if we allow it. We can close off the access to the nasal cavity by raising the **soft palate** (also known as the **velum**), or allow air to go into the nasal cavity by lowering it. The extreme end of the velum is a small piece of tissue called the **uvula** (you can see it by looking into the back of your mouth in a mirror—it is not a pretty sight), which plays a part in the pronunciation of some languages. Inside the mouth there are many parts which are used in speaking. The most obvious one is the tongue, which is so important in speaking that in many languages the word for 'language' is also the word for 'tongue'. It is amazingly mobile and flexible: consider, for example, how far you can push your tongue outside your mouth (some people can touch the tip of their nose with the tip of their tongue). This is done with muscles, yet muscles can only pull, not push. The tongue can move upwards and downwards, forwards and backwards. In producing vowels, the tongue does not make a great deal of contact with the **palate** (the upper surface of the mouth, sometimes called the 'roof' of the mouth); in many consonants, there is extensive contact. The lower jaw can also move upwards and downwards, and to a small extent forwards and backwards too. The teeth can be important in speaking, though we can't move them.

The outer end of the vocal tract is formed by the lips, which like the tongue, are very flexible and manoeuvrable. They can be moved towards each together and firmly closed, or can be moved further apart. They can be pushed forwards and rounded, or pulled back and widened as in a smile.

Describing speech production

Now that the various parts of the vocal tract have been introduced, let us look in detail at an example of how a word is produced. We will take the word 'sand'. You should read the description and see if it agrees with how you feel you say it. You will certainly find it strange to think of such a simple bit of speech requiring so many actions and such careful coordination. In speaking normally, we never have to think about what we are doing. It is very different for people recovering from a stroke, when with the help of a speech therapist they have to re-learn how to make even simple speech sounds.

You would probably take a breath before starting to speak, since there has to be enough air in your lungs to produce speech. The velum is then raised so that air cannot escape through the nose. The first sound, /s/, is made with the vocal folds apart and not vibrating. The air passes up through the larynx and the pharynx and into the mouth. Here it meets an obstacle: the front part of the tongue has been raised so that it is touching the roof of the mouth just behind the upper front teeth. This obstruction does not block the escape of air completely, but it forces the air to pass through a narrow gap and hit the teeth, making a hissing noise. The next sound is /æ/, and for this your vocal folds must be vibrating. So to move from /s/ to /æ/, you must bring the vocal folds together until they are in contact with each other, or nearly so. At the same time the tongue must be lowered so that it is no longer obstructing the flow of air. To produce an /æ/ sound the tongue must be quite low in the mouth, and the jaw is usually lowered. The velum is still raised to prevent the escape of air, but as you approach the /n/ sound which follows, the velum must be lowered, and this begins to happen towards the end of the /æ/. To make the /n/, the tongue and jaw must be raised into almost the same position it was in for making the initial /s/ sound, but this time the closure between the tongue and the roof of the mouth is complete. The vocal folds continue to vibrate, but now, with the velum lowered and the escape through the mouth blocked, all the flow of air passes through the nasal cavity and escapes through the nostrils. The final sound is /d/. The move from /n/ to /d/ is a very simple one: remember that during the /n/, the air is escaping through the nasal cavity and no escape of air is possible through the mouth. You now raise your velum (most people are not aware of doing this when they speak), and the escape of air through the nasal cavity is stopped. The flow of air stops and the vocal folds soon stop vibrating. This raising of the velum results in the /d/ sound. Once this has been done, it is necessary to return to the position for normal breathing (you would not live very long if you stayed making the /d/ sound and did not start the flow of air again). The vocal folds are moved apart, and both the tongue and the velum are lowered, so that air can flow freely into and out of the lungs.

This description sounds very complicated; it may help in understanding the process to read through the diagram in Figure 2.2. We have looked at just four speech sounds: /s/, /n/, and /d/ are consonant sounds, while /æ/ is a vowel. Although most people have heard of vowels and consonants, they usually find it difficult to say what the difference is. In phonetics, the essential difference is that consonants make some obstruction to the flow of air, while vowels make relatively little obstruction. This means that if you produce alternate consonants and vowels (as in the word 'potato'), your vocal tract is changing from closed to open, open to closed alternately. However, although the consonants in 'potato' are clearly different from vowels, there are quite a lot of cases where the difference is not so easy to see, and the readings for this chapter reflect some of the different ways of dealing with this problem.

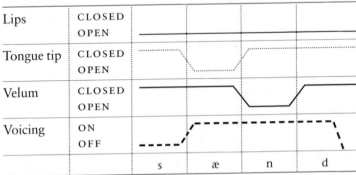

FIGURE 2.2 *Diagram of articulator movements for the word 'sand'*

3

Classifying speech sounds

Our articulators enable us to make an infinite number of different speech sounds, but in our scientific study we need some way of bringing order into the apparent chaos of all these different sounds. We have already seen how the most fundamental division we make (and have made for thousands of years) is between vowels and consonants. Within each of these basic categories, we can make finer and finer distinctions. It is interesting to compare our science with another such as botany. The world is full of plants of amazing variety, and each of them must be put into a scientific category; to do this requires a taxonomy of plants, a framework for classification. If a new plant is discovered, a botanist will try to decide whether it belongs within an existing family group, or whether a new class must be created. We do the same with the great variety of speech sounds we find being used in the world's languages.

For each language we examine, we are able to identify a number of **phonemes** (introduced in Chapter 1) which function in that particular language as distinctive—they work to distinguish meanings of different words in the language. The difference between the phonemes /p/ and /b/ in English causes us to hear the difference between the words 'pin' and 'bin'; the difference between /ɪ/ and /æ/ makes the difference between 'bit' and 'bat'. In the theory of the phoneme, the phoneme is abstract (like a letter of the alphabet), and what you hear is the **realization** of the phoneme—its physical form. Phonemes can have several different physical forms, or **allophones**.

When we have decided what category a sound belongs in, we can represent it with a symbol. Some symbols have already been introduced, but there are many more. As explained in Chapter 1, it is a long-established convention that when one wishes to distinguish between symbols for the phonemes of a particular language and IPA symbols for allophones, or for sounds in general, one should put the symbols between different brackets. Phoneme symbols should be between slant brackets: /e/, /s/ and so on; phonetic symbols should be between square brackets: [ø], [ɡ]. As an example, we will look at the word 'ostrich'. We can write this relatively simply in phonemic transcription as /ɒstrɪtʃ/; however, we might want to be more precise about the exact pronunciation. The /r/ is usually a voiceless sound in this context and can be represented phonetically as [ɹ̥]. Most English speakers have rounded lips for /tʃ/, which is therefore transcribed phonetically as [tʃʷ]; they also tend to put a glottal stop [ʔ] in front of /tʃ/, though this sound is not a phoneme of English. A phonetic transcription of 'ostrich', then could look like this: [ɒstɹ̥ɪʔtʃʷ].

When all the classification possibilities available to phoneticians have been listed, they can be put together in the form of a chart, the best-known of which is the **IPA** (International Phonetic Association) Chart. This is reproduced in Table 1.2 on pages 8–9.

Vowels

We have already looked briefly at vowels in the previous chapter. It has been claimed that the most basic vowels are [i] (similar to the vowel in the English word 'key') and [ɑ] (as in 'half'): similar vowels are found in the great majority of the world's languages, and they are the vowels that babies learn first. They are also different in one very important way: in [i], the tongue is close to the palate, while in [ɑ] the mouth is open, with the tongue low in the mouth. You can see the difference if you look in a mirror while saying these two sounds, one after the other. We therefore class [i] as a **close** vowel and [ɑ] as an **open** vowel.

We can find another very basic vowel: its symbol is [u]. Although the English vowel in 'who' is a reasonable example, we can find clearer cases in some other languages: the vowel in French 'vous', German 'du', or Spanish 'tu'. The [u] vowel differs from [i] in two important ways. The one which is easiest to observe is that the lips are rounded in [u], but unrounded or spread (as for a smile) in [i]. More difficult to observe is that the back of the tongue is raised for [u] while in [i] it is the front of the tongue which is raised. As a result, we say that [i] is a **front** vowel, while [u] is a **back** vowel.

By looking at these three vowels, we have seen the most import-ant features used for classifying vowels: a vowel may be close or open; front or back; rounded or unrounded. We can now look at where other vowels fit in this scheme—there are many different vowels in the world's languages, and we need to be able to put them in their place. On the open/close scale, we place two inter-mediate levels: mid-close and mid-open. In between front and back, we put central. At each point on the outside of the diagram we place two symbols: the left-hand item of each pair is unround-ed, while the one on the right is rounded. There is a well-known diagram used to represent the vowel 'space', known as the Cardinal Vowel Diagram. This can be seen in Figure 3.1.

The vowels that we place on this diagram are **cardinal vowels**, and these are not the vowels of any particular language. Indeed, there is some doubt about whether one of these vowels, [œ], has ever been observed as a phoneme in any language in the world, but it is nevertheless a vowel which we are capable of making, so we give it a symbol and a place on the diagram (in fact, the near-est sound to this rare beast that you are likely to hear is the sound of someone yawning loudly). Given this way of classifying vowels, we can give any vowel a phonetic label by describing its frontness, openness, and rounding: thus, using cardinal vowels as examples, we can say that [i] is a front close unrounded vowel, while [u] is a back close rounded vowel. The vowel [e] is a front mid-close unrounded vowel, while [ɔ] is a back mid-open rounded vowel.

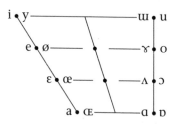

FIGURE 3.1 *The cardinal vowels*

There are many other ways in which vowels differ from each other, though the features we have looked at in this section are the most important ones. Some languages have nasalized vowels in addition to normal ones; in these, some of the air-flow is allowed to escape through the nose. French is a well-known example—the vowels in 'fin', 'bon', 'dans', and 'brun' are nasalized. Among other European languages, Portuguese and Polish also have nasalized vowels. There are also differences in vowel length, and some languages contrast long and short vowels. It has been claimed (but not accepted by everyone) that the Estonian language distinguishes short, medium and long vowel and consonant phonemes.

Consonants

As we saw in Chapter 2, all true consonants are the result of obstructing the flow of air through the vocal tract. When we classify consonants, we look at the following characteristics:

1 Whether the sound is **voiced** or **voiceless**.
2 The **place** (or places) **of articulation** where the obstruction is made.
3 The **manner of articulation** or type of obstruction.
4 The **airstream** used to make the consonant.

In the following examples slant brackets are used for transcriptions of English phonemes, and square brackets for allophones of English and other examples.

1 Voicing is sometimes seen as a binary (yes/no) matter—a sound is either voiced or it isn't. It is 'in fact' rather more complex than this—some sounds are voiced for only part of their time. For example, in English, the phonemes /b/, /d/, and /g/ (these are consonants of the type called **plosives**) often occur at the beginning of a word; although they are classed as voiced, the voicing usually begins only just before the end of the consonant. When the same consonants occur at the end of a word, we find the reverse: /b/, /d/, and /g/ have some

voiced plosives 'bin' /bɪn/; 'din' /dɪn/; 'go' /gəʊ/

other voiced consonants 'may' /meɪ/; 'no' /nəʊ/; 'low' /ləʊ/

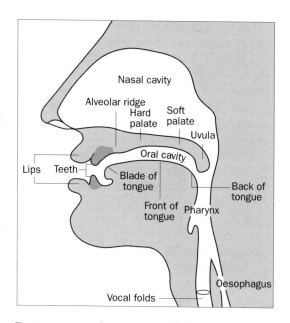

FIGURE 3.2 *Places of articulation*

voicing at the beginning, but then this dies away. Often the 'voiced' English **fricatives** /v/, /z/, and /ʒ/ behave in much the same way. Compared with these, other sounds such as /m/, /n/, and /l/ usually display full voicing, as do [b], [d], [g] in many other languages.

voiced fricatives 'van' /væn/; 'zoo' /zuː/; 'measure' /meʒə/

2 Place of articulation. We have already seen in the preceding chapter how consonants are made, and the relevant articulators can be seen in Figure 3.2. In the descriptions that follow, the examples are from BBC English unless otherwise specified.

We need to look in more detail at the vocal tract and its **articulators** in order to identify the places, and this can be seen in Figure 3.2. Starting from the outer end of the vocal tract, we have the lips, which give us the **bilabial**

bilabial 'bin' /bɪn/; 'pin' /pɪn/; 'man' /mæn/

labiodental 'fan' /fæn/; 'van' /væn/

dental 'think' /θɪŋk/; 'that' /ðæt/

alveolar 'tin' /tɪn/; 'din' /dɪn/; 'sin' /sɪn/; 'zip' /zɪp/; 'lip' /lɪp/; 'nip' /nɪp/

post-alveolar 'ship' /ʃɪp/; 'measure' /meʒə/

palatal English 'yet' /jet/; Italian 'figlio' [fiʎo]; 'ogni' [oɲi]; Hungarian 'Magyar' [mɑɟɑr]

velar 'cap' /kæp/; 'gap' /gæp/; 'sing' /sɪŋ/

uvular Dutch 'gat' [χɑt]; French 'rouge' [ʁuʒ]

pharyngeal Arabic [ħamm], [ʕala]

glottal 'hat' /hæt/, Cockney 'better' [beʔə]

retroflex Hindi [ʈal], [ɖal]

place of articulation. Behind these are the front teeth; if the lower lip touches the upper front teeth, we have a **labiodental** place, while if the tongue touches the teeth, the place is **dental**.

Behind the upper front teeth is the **alveolar ridge**, and if the tongue is in contact with this, the place is **alveolar**. The tongue can make contact with the upper surface of the mouth a little further back than the alveolar region, giving a **post-alveolar** place, while moving further back in the vocal tract brings us to the **palatal** area. Looking now at the back part of the mouth, we can see the velum. When the back of the tongue is in contact with this, the place is **velar**.

If the contact is further back, with contact against the extreme lower end of the velum, the place is **uvular**.

Moving downwards towards the larynx, we can see the pharynx, and if we constrict this we get a **pharyngeal** place. A constriction between the vocal folds, inside the larynx, has a **glottal** place of articulation, since the space between the vocal folds is known as the glottis.

In addition to these places in the mouth, there is another characteristic of some sounds which is traditionally classed as a place of articulation: this is **retroflex**. In a retroflex sound, the front part of the tongue is curled backwards so that if it makes contact with the upper surface of the mouth, it is the tip of the tongue, or even the underside, which makes contact. Consonants of this sort are commonly found in languages of the Indian subcontinent. 'Retroflex' is not really a place, but a shape of the tongue, and does not really belong in any of the normal categories of sound classification. Retroflexion is found also in vowels—it is often heard in the speech of Americans in vowels where there is an 'r' in the spelling, such as 'car', 'more', 'bird'.

3 Manner of articulation. Here we have to describe the type of obstruction to the airflow that is formed. This can range from a complete closure of the vocal tract, which prevents any air from escaping, to an articulation which in most ways is identical to that of a vowel. A **plosive** is a consonant which stops air from escaping. A closure is made at some point in the vocal tract, and air is compressed behind this. There is a brief period of complete, or almost complete, silence, and then the compressed air is released. When this air is released, there is a very short explosive noise, called **plosion**. This may be followed by a [h]-like sound known as **aspiration**.

> **plosives** 'pie' /paɪ/; 'buy' /baɪ/; 'tie' /taɪ/; 'die' /daɪ/; 'come' /kʌm/; 'gum' /gʌm/

A **nasal** consonant involves a complete closure in the oral cavity, but air is allowed to escape through the nose, since the velum is lowered for the production of this type of consonant.

> **nasals** 'map' /mæp/; 'nap' /nap/; 'hang' /hæŋ/

A **fricative** requires a constriction which allows the air to escape with difficulty, so that a hissing sound is produced. An **affricate** is a consonant which starts as a plosive, but instead of ending with plosion, ends with a fricative made in the same place.

> **fricatives** 'fin' /fɪn/; 'thin' /θɪn/; 'sin' /sɪn/; 'shin' /ʃɪn/; 'hint' /hɪnt/; 'vat' /væt/; 'that' /ðæt/; 'zip' /zɪp/; 'pleasure' /pleʒə/

> **affricates** 'church' /tʃɜːʧ/; 'judge' /dʒʌdʒ/

There is a class of sounds which are very brief: **tap** and **flap**. To make a tap, the tongue is briefly flicked up against the roof of the mouth, interrupting the flow of air for a short time. A flap is similar, but the tongue is curled back and then flicked forward against the alveolar ridge. An unusual and difficult sound is the **trill**. Various articulators are mobile enough to vibrate if the air-flow is suitable.

> **tap** Spanish 'pero' [peɾo]; Italian 'caro' [karo]
> **trill** Spanish 'perro' [pero]; Italian 'carro' [karo]
> **flap** Hindi [beɽɑ]; Hausa [báɽà]

The tongue-tip and the uvula are suitable for trilling and are used for this in a number of languages. If you trill your lips, you produce what is sometimes called a 'raspberry' or, in America, a 'Bronx cheer'.

Finally, there is a class of sounds which are collectively called **approximants**. One of these is the **lateral**: in this type, the centre of the tongue is in close contact with the roof of the mouth, but the sides of the tongue are lowered so that air can escape along the sides of the tongue. A **post-alveolar** approximant is a rather vague concept, but the term is normally used to refer to the 'r' sound of the English of America and England, where the tongue is slightly curled backwards but does not make contact with the upper surface of the mouth.

lateral approximant 'led' /led/; 'hill' /hɪl/
post-alveolar approximants 'red' [ɹed]; 'hurry' [hʌɹi]; American English 'car' [kɑɹ] 'cart' [kɑɹt]

4 Airstream mechanism. Finally, we should (if we are being as precise as possible) also specify the airstream mechanism of a consonant: it may be **pulmonic**, made by the movement of air out of or (much more rarely) into the lungs, **glottalic**, made by moving air inwards or outwards by lowering or raising the larynx in the throat, or **velaric**, made by making a velar closure (as for [k] or [g]) and sliding the tongue backwards or forwards to move air inwards or outwards. When the air is moved outwards, we call it **egressive**, while inward movement is called **ingressive**.

Having established these principal ways of classifying consonants, we can make up labels which define any given consonant. We will assume for now that we are looking at egressive pulmonic consonants (made with air expelled from the lungs).

[s] is a voiceless alveolar fricative
[g] is a voiced velar plosive
[l] is a voiced alveolar lateral approximant
[tʰ] is a voiceless aspirated alveolar plosive.

These labels are important in phonetics for specifying a sound in an unambiguous way, but it can take a long time to learn how to use them properly.

4

Tone and tone languages

We have seen in Chapter 2 that we are able to control the **pitch** of our voice. In this chapter we look at one of the most important functions of this pitch control. We will begin with a simple example. In the following examples, the words are given in phonetic transcription and each has a diagram of the pitch that is produced, with the upper line representing the highest pitch of the speaker, and the lower line the lowest pitch. We will not use square brackets for these examples, for the sake of clarity. The words are from Kono (Sierra Leone).

‾kɔɔ 'to mature'   _kɔɔ 'rice'

FIGURE 4.1 *Example of pitch level distinguishing a word*

Note that both words contain exactly the same segments, but they are different in pitch. In some cases it is the pitch level that distinguishes a word, while in others it is a pitch movement. We refer to these characteristics of pitch as **tone**. Each word in the above example has a distinctive tone. One of the interesting facts about languages is that some use tone in this distinctive way, while others (including most European languages) do not. Languages which use tone distinctively are called **tone languages**. It is probably true to say that the majority of the world's population speaks a tone language, so it is surprising how little importance is given to this aspect of speech in books on phonetics. Perhaps this shows that the subject is dominated by speakers of European languages. We find tone languages in South-East Asia (for example,

Chinese, Thai, and Vietnamese), in much of south and west Africa (for example, Hausa, Yoruba, and Zulu), and in indigenous languages of America (for example, Mixteco, Zapotec, Navajo).

Lexical and grammatical use of tone

Tone works in different ways in different languages. The easiest to explain is what we can call *lexical tone*, where the meaning of a word (as it would appear in a dictionary) is determined by its tone. So in Vietnamese, whose writing system is based on the Roman alphabet, vowels are represented with additional marks which indicate one of the language's six tones. Two of the tones, known as 'broken' tones, are (in the Northern dialect) accompanied by glottalization (rather like a rapid glottal stop in the middle of the **syllable**). A Vietnamese dictionary has to list the different words with their tones. The marks, and the tones they represent, are as follows:

1 Mid-level (no mark). Example: a
2 Low falling (grave accent). Example: à
3 High rising (acute accent). Example: á
4 Low, rising after dip (circle). Example: å
5 High 'broken' (tilde). Example: ã
6 Low 'broken' (subscript dot). Example: ạ

In some languages, tone may function as a way of showing different aspects of grammar. In Kono, the following sentences differ only in the use of high and low tones (shown by the tone-marks placed before each syllable in the transcription):

_a _a ⁻do _ma _ko   'Wash his shirt'

_a ⁻a _do ⁻ma _ko   'He has washed a shirt'

Tone levels and contours

In the phonetic study of tone, we are not just concerned with the meaning of tones, but with the physical nature of their sounds. In some tone languages, the most important thing about the tones is the difference between tone levels: whether the pitch is high or low. Some languages distinguish only high and low, while others may have as many as four different levels. Each speaker will have their own individual pitch level for high and low, and for the tones in between, so the important thing is the difference between the tones rather than the exact pitch of the tone. In other languages, however, the important difference is between the shapes of the tones rather than the levels—tones can have rising pitch, falling pitch, falling–rising, or rising–falling, as well as level. It has been claimed for a long time that there is a fundamental difference between these two types of tone language (they are sometimes called *register* and *contour* tone languages), but there are many cases where it is difficult to decide which of the two types a language belongs to, so the distinction does not seem to be very useful.

Tones and context

Most speakers who do not speak a tone language would find it relatively easy to study tone if it were not for the fact that tones tend to vary in ways that are very difficult to predict, according to the context in which they occur. The story is told of a missionary who felt he had a vocation to work in West Africa, but when he discovered the difficulty of learning the tones of the local language he decided that he must have made a mistake in hearing the call from the Lord. Even if one can successfully recognize the individual tones of a tone language in words spoken in isolation, the tonal characteristics of those words may become very different when they occur in connected speech. Around two thousand years ago, Sanskrit grammarians in India made detailed studies of the effects of context on speech sounds, and gave the term **sandhi** to these effects. In *tonal* sandhi, a tone is modified by the tones of neighbouring syllables. An example is found in Mandarin Chinese, in which the tones are numbered as follows:

1 high level   (e.g. ¯ma 'mother')
2 high rising   (e.g. /ma 'hemp')
3 falling-rising (e.g. ∨ma 'horse')
4 high falling   (e.g. \ma 'scold')

However, when a syllable carrying tone 3 is followed by another tone 3 syllable, the first syllable's tone changes to tone 2. When a tone 2 syllable is preceded by a tone 1 or tone 2, and is followed by a stressed syllable, it becomes a tone 1. This does not make life any easier for someone learning Chinese. To add to the complexity, there are other effects such as **downdrift**, where, as an utterance goes on, the tones in the utterance become gradually lower and lower until the speaker reaches the end of a sentence, or pauses for breath. This means that a low tone found at the beginning of an utterance might have the same pitch as a high tone syllable at the end of the utterance. There is yet another effect found, different from downdrift, which is **downstep**. In this case, a high tone when it occurs on a syllable between other tone-bearing syllables is pronounced on a lower pitch than it would have in isolation—this could be regarded as a special case of tonal sandhi.

Tones and pitch-accents

Nobody has ever claimed that English is a tone language. However, pitch and pitch movements play an important role in English and similar languages in marking out certain syllables as distinctive and important. If you say the word 'important' on its own, you will probably notice that on the middle syllable the pitch of your voice steps up from the pitch of the first syllable, then glides down to the lower pitch of the final syllable. This distinctive pitch movement is sometimes known as **accent**, and the middle syllable can be said to be accented. It is not always easy to distinguish this function of pitch from the tonal contrasts that we have been looking at earlier in this chapter. In a number of languages which are not normally thought of as tone languages it is possible to find pairs of words which really seem to be distinguished from each other by pitch characteristics. One example is the following pair of Japanese words.

hási (meaning 'chopstick')   hasí (meaning 'bridge')

As the pitch diagrams show, these are distinguished by whether the pitch moves from high to low (as in the first word) or from low to high. Here is an example from Swedish:

anden ('duck')   anden ('spirit')

These are distinguished by the fact that in one, the pitch falls from high to low on the first syllable and remains low on the second, while in the other the pitch of each syllable falls from high to low. Similar examples can be found in Serbo-Croat.

In a tone language, pitch variation is used on practically all the syllables or words of the language, but in the cases just mentioned, only a limited number of words are distinguished by pitch. To avoid having to class Japanese, Swedish, Norwegian, and Serbo-Croat as tone languages, we say that they are pitch-accent languages, and that certain words are distinguished by pitch-accents.

5

Suprasegmentals

In tone languages, it is usually relatively easy to see the function of the different tones. However, in languages which do not use tone in this way, it is harder to explain what we are doing when we make use of changes in pitch, loudness, and other **suprasegmental features** of speech. There are several such features: what they all have in common is that we usually see them as properties of pieces of speech which will be at least as long as one syllable, and may extend for many words. So if, for example, I say 'no' loudly, it is most likely that both the /n/ sound and the /əʊ/ will be loud. If I say 'hurry' quickly, then all the phonemes of that word will be said quickly. The most important suprasegmental features of speech are pitch, loudness, **tempo** (that is, speed), and **voice quality**, but these are by no means the only ones. The study of these features is often referred to as the study of **prosody**. Two such features form the basis for specially important functions, **stress** and **intonation**.

Stress and accent

In any language you listen to, you will notice that some syllables sound stronger and more noticeable than others. In English, for example, the middle syllable of the word 'tomato' is clearly stronger than the first and last syllables. We say that the middle syllable is *stressed*. In some languages the position of the strongest stress may affect the meaning of a word. The following Spanish words are shown with the stressed syllables underlined, and their meanings are given:

término 'terminus'
termino 'I terminate'
terminó 'I terminated'

English has some pairs of semantically related words whose grammatical category is reflected in their stress pattern, such as:

import (noun)
import (verb)

There are other pairs of words where the difference in stress signals functions in other ways: in the pair 'subject'/'subject', the two words differ in grammatical category (noun/verb) but seem in some contexts to be unrelated semantically; the pair 'recall'/'recall', however, may have the same grammatical category (both may be nouns) and be semantically related. In some other languages, it is possible to hear the difference between stressed and unstressed syllables, but the stress usually falls in the same position in a word of more than one syllable. In French, it is usual for stress to fall on the final syllable of the word, while in Polish it is usually on the penultimate syllable (the syllable before last), with a few exceptions such as 'uniwersytet' ('university'). In languages such as these, we cannot say that stress is able to determine the meaning of a word. We may guess that stress performs a different function: it helps us to divide the continuous flow of speech into separate words. For example, if I am listening to someone speaking French, I know that when I hear a stressed syllable, that is the last syllable of a word. One of the great unsolved mysteries of speech perception is how we manage to divide continuous speech up into separate words in languages like English (in which stress gives us relatively little help).

A number of factors cause a syllable to be made prominent so that it is heard as stressed. In English, stressed syllables are usually louder and longer than unstressed syllables, and have distinctive pitch (as in the example of the word 'important' given in the previous chapter). We can detect different levels of stress in words of several syllables. Try saying to yourself the four-syllable English word 'understanding': the strongest stress should be heard on the third syllable, but the second and fourth syllables are much weaker than the first syllable. Usually, only the third syllable has a noticeably distinct pitch.

Distinctive pitch, such as we find on the third syllable of 'understanding', is given special importance in the study of stress in English, and the term **accent**, which was introduced in the previous chapter, is used to refer to it. Consider now how you would say the phrase 'understanding English': you will probably find that there is no longer a noticeable pitch movement on the third syllable of 'understanding', but there is one on the first syllable of 'English'. The 'stand' syllable is still quite prominent, but it isn't accented. The word *stressed* can be retained for syllables (such as 'un' and 'stand' in this example) which are made prominent by other features such as length or loudness. This property is known as **stress**. The same distinction can be made in most other languages in which stress and accent play linguistically important roles.

Intonation

Intonation has always been a difficult thing to define. According to traditional descriptions, intonation is 'the melody of speech', and is to be analysed in terms of variations in pitch. We have seen, in the chapter on tone, how changes in pitch can change meaning, but in the case of intonation the way meaning is changed is not so clear. If we look at a typical example, we would expect a falling pitch pattern on a statement like this:

You're   from   London

but a rising pitch pattern if the same words are used as a question:

You're   from   London?

Intonation can, then, indicate different types of utterance, such as statements and questions. Other examples of meaning being changed by differences in intonation are often quoted: the difference between

She won't go out with anyone

and

She won't go out with anyone

is that the first one (with a falling pitch movement on 'any') says that she will go out with nobody, while the second (with a falling-rising pitch movement) says that she is careful about who she goes out with. In the case of

I have plans to leave

I am saying that I have some diagrams or drawings to leave, while

I have plans to leave

means that I am planning to leave.

Intonation also gives the listener a lot of information about what is being said. In the English of South-East England, a lot of use is made of a falling-rising intonation pattern: for example, it is often used for polite requests:

Can you lend me some money?

and for expressing reservation:

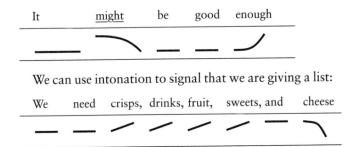

We can use intonation to signal that we are giving a list:

Intonation is said to indicate the attitudes and emotions of the speaker, so that a sentence like 'I think it's time to go now' can be said in a happy way, a sad way, an angry way, and so on. While this is certainly true, there is clearly more than just pitch variation involved in conveying such things, so the definition of intonation becomes considerably more complicated. It is clear that when we are expressing emotions, we also use different voice qualities, different speaking rates, facial expressions, gestures, and so on. What can we conclude about the use of intonation in a language like English? Although examples like those above can be produced which suggest functions related to the grammar of an utterance and the psychological state of the speaker, these seem to show only part of the picture. Perhaps the best way to look at the subject is to see intonation as an essential component of the **discourse** structure of speech. We speak in order to communicate, and we need to interact with our listeners to do this. We must indicate what type of information we are presenting and how it is structured, and at the same time we must keep our listeners' attention and their participation in the exchange of information. Communicative interaction would be much more difficult without intonation: think how many misunderstandings between people arise in the exchange of e-mail messages, where intonation cannot play a role.

It is difficult to work out a satisfactory way of transcribing intonation. In the examples given above, a 'wiggly-line' representation of the pitch movement is given, but although this helps to

explain the examples, it does not indicate which bits of intonation are significant. The problem lies in the fact that intonation
is claimed to be meaningful and contrastive in a similar way to
the tones of a tone language. In the latter case, we know that we
can represent the tones with a set of marks which correspond to
the contrastive tones of the language. But it is much more difficult
to decide how to divide intonation up into contrastive units, and
many different ways have been proposed. In much British work
on intonation, a transcription system is used which places marks
in the text to indicate the important features:

We need / crisps / drinks / fruit / sweets and \ cheese

Rhythm

There are many parallels between speech and music, and one thing
that is always found in music is **rhythm**. In music, the rhythm is
usually produced by making certain notes in a sequence stand out
from others by being louder or longer or higher. We should not
make the mistake of thinking that musical rhythm is just an un-
varying repetition of beats at equal intervals. This may be true of
commercial pop music (as can be heard coming out of someone's
headphones, or through the wall from the room next door), but
throughout the world in traditional folk music and other serious
musical forms we can find some amazingly complex rhythms
which are still immediately recognizable as regular. In speech, we
find that syllables take the place of musical notes or beats, and in
many languages the stressed syllables determine the rhythm. If
you were asked to clap your hands in time with the sentence

'This is the 'first 'time I've 'ever 'eaten a 'chocolate 'caterpillar

you would be most likely to clap at the points marked with the
stress mark '. It is often claimed that English speakers try to keep
an equal time between the stressed syllables, so the time between
claps of your hands would be quite regular. Rhythm of this type is
called **stress-timed**, and it is claimed that the unstressed syllables
between the stressed syllables are squeezed into the time available, with the result that they may become very short. In fact, this

is only found in a style of speech (slow, emphatic) where the rhythm is strong, and in ordinary conversational speech it is much harder to make a convincing case for this **isochronous** rhythm (where the time intervals between stressed syllables are equal); as with music, we should not expect rhythm to be simple. Other languages have different rhythms (as you can easily hear by listening to them). To the ears of English speakers, Italian and Swedish have a very different rhythm from English. Spanish, French, and Chinese sound **syllable-timed** to English-speaking listeners—it sounds as though all the syllables are of equal length, and the dominant role of stressed syllables in making up the rhythm is much less noticeable. But these judgements are very subjective, and finding scientific evidence about what makes us hear languages as rhythmically different is proving to be very difficult. What does seem to be clear is that rhythm is useful to us in communicating: it helps us to find our way through the confusing stream of continuous speech, enabling us to divide speech into words or other units, to signal changes between topic or speaker, and to spot which items in the message are the most important.

Other suprasegmental features

It is possible to analyse the suprasegmental side of speech in great detail and to discover more features that vary as we speak. Some have been mentioned already: the speed or **tempo** of speaking is certainly something that we all can and do change, as is the loudness. **Voice quality** may vary from soft and gentle to harsh and unpleasant. Many of these features of speech are believed to be important in communication, but to have only a weak connection with the linguistic structure and phonology of the language since it is almost impossible to decide what is contrasted with what. They are therefore sometimes called **paralinguistic features**. These are very interesting in the study of how we behave when we speak to other people, particularly in the case of the expression of emotions. Even if you can't see the person who is speaking, you can detect emotions like anger, fear, happiness, or disgust in their voice. If we want to understand how this works, it certainly won't be sufficient to describe only the movements of the speaker's pitch, as traditional intonation textbooks have done. We need a much more complex framework of features and descriptive labels, covering all aspects of the voice. At present we simply do not know in any detail what is happening when a particular emotion is conveyed, despite all the research being carried out.

6
Acoustics of speech sounds

When we speak to each other the sounds we make have to travel from the mouth of the speaker to the ear of the listener. This is true whether we are speaking face to face, or by telephone over thousands of miles. What is important for us in our study of speech is that this acoustic signal is completely observable: we can capture everything that the listener hears in the form of a recording, and then measure whichever aspect of the signal that we want to know about. There is an interesting observation to make here: for each of the phonetic classes of sound that we have identified, we can find corresponding acoustic patterns. However, if we had started by studying the types of acoustic pattern without knowing anything about how they were made by a human speaker, we would probably have set up a quite different way of classifying them. We will begin by setting out a classification of acoustic patterns, and then see how this fits with the traditional phonetic classification of speech sounds.

Acoustic waveforms

All audible sound is the result of variations in air pressure that produce vibration. In vibration, the pressure in a particular place (for example, inside the ear) becomes alternately higher and lower. This is usually described in terms of wave motion, using diagrams like Figure 6.1 that suggest up-and-down movement, though sound waves do not really move up and down like waves on the sea. They are more like the shock waves that travel outwards from an explosion. We can show the pattern of a particular sort of vibration by displaying its **waveform**. If the vibration

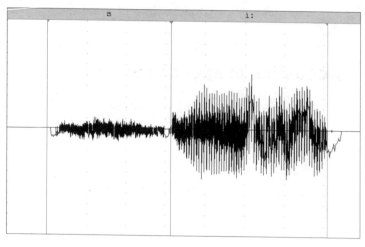

FIGURE 6.1 *Acoustic waveform of 'see'.* /siː/

happens rapidly, we say it has a high **frequency**, and if it happens less rapidly, we say it has a lower frequency. If the vibration is regular, repeating its pattern over and over, we call the sound **periodic**, while a pattern of vibration which does not have such a pattern of regular vibration is called aperiodic. If the sound contains a large amount of energy, we say that it has high **amplitude**. Figure 6.1 shows the waveform for the word 'see'; the first part, /s/, is **aperiodic**, having an irregular, rather messy pattern, while the vowel /iː/ is periodic, and we can see a more regular pattern in its vibration.

It is a fundamental principle in acoustic analysis that any waveform, however complex it might be, can be broken down into simple waveforms of different frequencies. The operation of doing this is called **spectral analysis**, and in some ways is rather like breaking down white light into the rainbow pattern of colours that make up its spectrum. In carrying out the acoustic analysis of speech sounds, we can discover much more by looking at the result of a spectral analysis than by looking at the original waveform that was captured by the microphone. Figure 6.2 shows the picture resulting from the spectral analysis of the word 'see' that we have already looked at in Figure 6.1. This type of picture is called a **spectrogram**. At one time there was a fashion

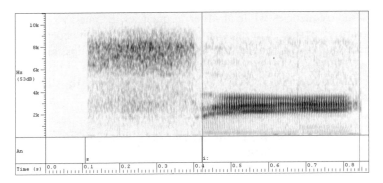

FIGURE 6.2 *Spectrogram of 'see'* /siː/

for calling such pictures 'voice-prints', but this led to some very dubious claims being made about identifying people by their voices for legal purposes, and the name is not now used except (sometimes) by gullible journalists.

In a spectrogram, the vertical axis of the picture represents the frequency scale: the lowest frequencies are shown at the bottom. From left to right is the time axis, with the beginning of the sound analysed shown at the left. The degree of blackness of the markings shows the amplitude at different frequencies in the signal at a particular point in time. You can see that in /s/ the energy is spread widely on the frequency range, but it is greater towards the higher frequencies and almost non-existent at the lowest frequencies. In /iː/, the energy is concentrated in three or four narrow bands (**formants**) in the lower part of the spectrum. Some spectrographic displays now show levels of energy with different colours instead, but although these look pretty and are nice to pin on your wall, most people find they are harder to interpret than the grey-scale spectrograms that have been around since the 1940s.

There is a general theory of how the acoustic signal is produced by the human vocal tract, based on the principle that we have some way of producing sound (a **source**), and for most sounds also a way of modifying that sound (a **filter**). This source–filter theory is widely accepted as a fundamental concept in speech acoustics. To take vowels as an example, the source for a vowel is the vibration of the vocal folds; as the vibrating flow of air passes through the vocal tract, the vocal tract acts as a filter, weakening the energy at some frequencies while at other frequencies the energy remains relatively strong. The shape of the vocal tract (which depends on factors like the tongue-shape, the position of the lips, and the position of the velum) determines the characteristics of this filter so that a particular vowel is produced; if you change the shape of the vocal tract, you change the resulting vowel.

Acoustic and articulatory classification of speech sounds

Now that we have seen something of the physical properties of sound, we can see how these properties correspond to our more familiar and traditional phonetic categories. We can say that all speech sounds are made up of just four possible types of acoustic pattern:

1 Periodic sound
2 Aperiodic sound
3 A mixture of periodic and aperiodic sound
4 Silence.

1 Vowels. These are periodic sounds with a regular pattern of vibration. When their spectrum is analysed, it is possible to see peaks of energy at different frequency, rather like the notes in a musical chord. These peaks of energy (which we call **formants**) are different for every vowel, and acoustic phoneticians have analysed the frequencies of many different vowels so that we know a lot about how formants are related to vowel quality. Formants are seen on spectrograms as dark horizontal bars, as in the /iː/ vowel that you can see in Figure 6.2. Although the relationship is certainly not exact, it has been found that the formant with the lowest frequency (Formant 1) corresponds roughly to the traditional open/close dimension of vowels: a low Formant 1 corresponds to a **close** vowel like [i] or [u]. Formant 2, which is higher than Formant 1, corresponds roughly to the front/back dimension of vowels: a vowel with a high Formant 2 is likely to be a **front** vowel like [e] or [a], while a vowel with a low Formant 2 is more likely to be a **back** vowel like [o] or [ɑ]. It is not possible to give exact frequency values for the different formants, because these vary from speaker to speaker, but the graph shown in Figure 6.3 places some English vowels spoken by an adult female speaker, with the axes arranged so that the positions of the vowels are roughly where they would be placed on a traditional vowel diagram. If you look carefully at textbooks which describe the acoustics of vowels, you will notice how depressingly often they assume that an adult male voice is 'normal' and give little or no detail of women's and children's voices.

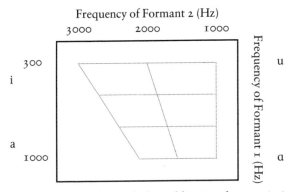

FIGURE 6.3 *Traditional (dotted line) and acoustic (solid line) representation of vowel positions*

2 Fricatives. Voiceless fricatives such as [s] and [ʃ] are aperiodic, and do not have formants in the way that vowels do. They do, however, have concentrations of energy at different frequencies. If you make [s] and [ʃ] alternately, you will hear that [s] sounds more high-pitched than [ʃ]. This is particularly noticeable in English, since English speakers tend to round their lips for /ʃ/, making this fricative sound even lower-pitched. You can check in a mirror whether you round your lips when you say an English /ʃ/. Voiced fricatives combine aperiodic with periodic sound. This is because they have the aperiodic hissing noise typical of voiceless fricatives such as [f], [s], or [ʃ], combined with vibration of the vocal folds. The vibration of the vocal folds happens in a very regular way, which means that the buzzing sound made in the larynx is periodic.

3 Plosives. Plosives occur in several different acoustic forms. We will begin by looking at voiceless plosives such as [p], [t], or [k]. Although most people are not aware of this, the first important component of these sounds is silence. When a voiceless plosive occurs at the beginning of a word (as in 'pin' /pɪn/), the word begins with a complete closure of the mouth, so that no air can escape, and during that time your lips are firmly pressed together for /p/ but no sound is made. If you think of a word like 'upper' /ʌpə/, it is clear that there must be a short silence in the middle of the word if a listener is to hear a /p/ sound there. When the closure is released, things start happening very rapidly as far as acoustic events are concerned. The release of the air causes a small explosion, and this sound is aperiodic—it is like a very brief fricative, and *transient*—it changes very rapidly. If the plosive is an aspirated one, as English /p/, /t/, and /k/ often are, this 'release burst' is followed by a different sound—the sound of air rushing through the vocal tract. This is called **aspiration** (which was introduced in Chapter 3), and is aperiodic (it is closely related to the [h] consonant).

Voiced plosives are periodic during the time that the vocal tract is closed; at this stage, instead of the silence that we find in voiceless plosives, we can hear (but only just) the vibration of the vocal folds coming from the larynx. Although we class English /b/, /d/, and /g/ as voiced plosives, they actually have very little voicing, so to hear a good example of a truly voiced plosive you should listen to some other languages: French, Spanish, and Italian are good examples.

4 Nasals. Nasal sounds such as English /m/, and /n/ are periodic. They are similar to vowels, but they have much less energy at higher frequencies and it is very difficult to identify formants in their spectrum. This is mainly because most of the sound generated in the larynx by the vibration of the vocal folds cannot escape out through the mouth as it does in the case of vowels, but has to pass through the nasal cavity and out through the nostrils. If you put your fingers in your ears and produce a sequence of vowel and nasal sounds like /maːmaːmaːmaː/ you will be able to hear the low-frequency humming sound created by the nasal resonance during the time that you are producing /m/.

5 **Affricates.** These are acoustically complex sounds. Voiceless affricates such as [tʃ] begin as plosives, so their initial portion is silence. After this, the closure in the vocal tract is released and we hear a fricative sound, which is aperiodic. Voiced affricates (if they are *really* voiced) are accompanied by vocal fold vibration; as a result, the first part is periodic and the second part is a mixture of periodic and aperiodic.

6 **Approximants.** As explained in Chapter 3, approximants are quite similar in their articulation to vowels. Not surprisingly, then, they are also *acoustically* similar to vowels. Sounds like [l], [r], [w], and [j] are periodic, and have recognizable formants (with the possible exception of [l], where the formants are sometimes hard to identify).

We have now looked at almost all the major classes of speech sound, and seen how each can be related to the major types of acoustic pattern. Only one group of sounds, the trills, flaps, and taps, remains to be examined. **Taps** and **flaps** (such as [ɾ] and [ɽ]) are usually voiced, and are therefore to be seen as being very brief voiced plosives. **Trills**, too, such as the tongue-tip trill [r] and the uvular trill [ʀ], are usually voiced, and we find the strange situation that these sounds are *doubly* periodic: they

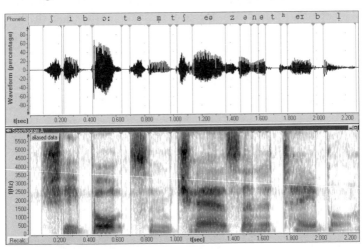

FIGURE 6.4 *Acoustic waveform and spectrogram of the sentence 'She bought some chairs and a table.'*

are periodic as a result of the vocal fold vibration, and also periodic because of the regular (though much slower) vibration of one of the articulators, such as the tongue-tip.

Figure 6.4 presents an acoustic waveform and a spectrogram of an English phrase ('She bought some chairs and a table') which contains examples of many of the above sounds.

Acoustics of suprasegmental features

Another aspect of acoustic phonetics is the analysis of the **suprasegmental features** of speech which were introduced in Chapter 5. When we hear the tones of a tone language, or the intonation of an utterance, we experience the sensation of **pitch**. This only happens in the case of voiced sounds. The sensation of pitch is related to the frequency of vocal fold vibration, which we call **fundamental frequency**. This means that we have one word (pitch) for a subjective sensation and another (fundamental frequency, or $F0$) for something that we can measure objectively. In a similar way, we can perceive the loudness of a sound or syllable, and we can also use instruments to measure its **intensity**; we perceive the length of a sound, and can measure its **duration**. Using computers to measure fundamental frequency and duration, we can discover a lot about such aspects of speech as intonation, stress, and rhythm.

7
Sounds in systems

We have seen in previous chapters how we can describe speech sounds, and classify them according to established frameworks. We must not forget, however, that we produce speech for a particular purpose — to communicate. We can only do this because speech sounds are used by speakers of a particular language according to its rules, and speech perception can only work by our being able to recognize these sounds. Each language has only a limited set (or system) of sounds that its speakers use. Each sound in the system must be distinctive: we must be able to show that the identity of a word can change if we substitute one phoneme for another. In addition, these sounds can only be combined in particular ways. It is interesting to look at how speech develops in children: in the child's earliest months of life, it makes a meaningless babble of noises that have little or no resemblance to the sounds of the language it is going to learn. But in a year or two from birth most of the strange sounds the baby makes will disappear from its speech for ever (unless it decides to study phonetics later in life), and the child will have learned the sounds and the patterns of sounds that are typical of the language. What is it that the child has learned? The short answer is to say that it has learned the **phonology** of its native language. The phonology of a language is part of its linguistic structure, which explains why phonology of the sort described here is sometimes called **linguistic phonetics**. The theoretical study of phonology involves far more than the rather basic observations about sound systems that are made in this chapter; to give a proper account of phonology would need a different book.

Systems of sounds

Space does not allow a detailed treatment of the different systems of contrasting sounds found in different languages, but the following brief survey shows some of the variety found in **vowel** and **consonant** systems.

Vowels

Many interesting observations have been made about the vowel systems of different languages; many are the subject of argument and competing interpretations. One question concerns the number of contrasting vowels that a language may have. Many of the world's languages have only three vowel phonemes, and these are almost always /i/ , /a/, and /u/. Many more have five, and these are most often the three above, plus /e/ and /o/. It seems that there are more odd-numbered than even-numbered vowel systems in the world. The lowest number is disputable, but there have been claims of languages with only two vowel phonemes, and a somewhat mythical one-vowel language. When we find a language with a large number of vowels, we usually find it possible to subdivide the vowels into categories. British English (**BBC accent**), for example, is claimed to have 20 vowels, usually divided into the following groups:

'Short vowels'	'Long vowels'	'Diphthongs'
ɪ	iː	eɪ
e	ɑː	aɪ
æ	ɜː	ɔɪ
ʌ	ɔː	aʊ
ɒ	uː	əʊ
ʊ		ɪə
ə		eə
		ʊə

TABLE 7.1 *Twenty vowels of 'British English'*

With a little ingenuity, this large number can be reduced to a much smaller system, for example by treating long vowels and **diphthongs** as being combinations of two phonemes. A six-vowel analysis of the English vowel system is possible. It might look something like this: we would have a set of six basic short vowels /i, e, a, o, ʌ, u/. The schwa vowel [ə] could be treated as an **allophone** of one or more of these vowels: one possibility that has been suggested is to say that [ʌ] and [ə] are, respectively, stressed and unstressed allophones of the same phoneme. Long vowels and diphthongs can be treated as pairs of short vowels: /ii, aa, uu/ for /iː, aː, uː/, for example. We are free to choose whichever analysis seems most suitable for our purposes.

Consonants

All languages have consonants, but their number and variety is very different from language to language. As with vowels, we tend to look for groups and patterns rather than overall lists. Some languages manage with very few consonants (less than a dozen, in some cases). Very few of the many Australian aboriginal languages have fricative consonants, yet almost all other languages have at least some. English has six plosive consonant phonemes (/p, t, k, b, d, g/), but many languages of India have more: Hindi, for example, has sixteen. They can be arranged like this:

PLOSIVE TYPE	PLACE OF ARTICULATION			
	Bilabial	*Dental*	*Retroflex*	*Velar*
Voiceless unaspirated	p	t̪	t	k
Voiceless aspirated	pʰ	t̪ʰ	tʰ	kʰ
Voiced unaspirated	b	d̪	ḍ	g
Voiced aspirated	bʰ	d̪ʰ	ḍʰ	gʰ

TABLE 7.2 *Plosive phonemes in Hindi*

English speakers find it difficult to learn to manage such a complicated set of contrasting plosives, but Hindi speakers apparently manage with no trouble. Another Indian language, Malayalam, contrasts bilabial, dental, alveolar, retroflex and velar places of articulation for plosives and nasals. The use of voicing and aspiration for making phonemic distinctions varies greatly among different languages: a few languages do not have a voiced/voiceless distinction at all. Korean does have voiced and voiceless consonants, but among its plosives there are no voiced plosives such as [b], [d], and [g]. There are voiceless plosives with (1) no aspiration, (2) weak aspiration, and (3) strong aspiration. We might represent this in table form as follows:

Place of articulation	Unaspirated	Weakly aspirated	Strongly aspirated
bilabial	p	p^h	ph
alveolar	t	t^h	th
velar	k	k^h	kh

TABLE 7.3 *Plosives and aspiration in Korean*

The great variety of the sound systems of the world's languages is one of the most fascinating aspects of phonetics and phonology. You can find out more about this subject in the Readings and References sections for this chapter.

Groups of sounds

Something else that varies from language to language is the way in which the sounds can be combined together. When this is studied, it is usually done in the context of syllable structure: if you can describe the form which syllables may take in a particular language, you are able to describe the possible combinations of phonemes. In many of the world's languages, the description is very simple: every consonant must be followed by a vowel, giving a syllable form that we can label CV (consonant+vowel), and the only other possible syllable is V (a vowel on its own). Japanese syllables are of this form. More complex syllable patterns might allow, for example, up to two consonants at the beginning of a syllable and up to one at the end: we find this in Spanish (the word 'tren' (train) is an example of a maximum syllable). English syllables may have three consonants at the beginning (in words like 'strong' /strɒŋ/, 'screw' /skruː/), and up to four at the end (in words like 'sixths' /sɪksθs/, 'texts' /teksts/). It is very important to note that the choice of which consonants and vowels can occur in syllables is not free: each language has quite firm restrictions on what is and what is not a real syllable of the language, and learning these 'rules' is part of learning the language. It isn't enough to say that Spanish syllables may have one consonant at the end: that consonant can only be one of a limited set of possible consonants.

English syllables may end with no consonant (as in 'me' /miː/), but this statement does not tell you everything you need to know, since most short vowels cannot occur in a syllable with no final consonant. You could not have an English word such as /te/, /tæ/, /tɒ/, or /tʌ/, and it is debatable whether /tɪ/ or /tʊ/ are possible, but it is perfectly possible to have 'open' syllables like this if the vowel is long: 'tea' /tiː/, 'tar' /tɑː/, 'tore' /tɔː/, 'too' /tuː/. The study of such patterns of sounds is part of the subject of phonology, and forms a very important part of the study of the sound systems of different languages.

8

Connected speech and coarticulation

We normally speak by producing a continuous, connected stream of sounds, except when we pause. In most languages we can find occasional cases where a speaker makes a single segment in isolation with no sound preceding or following it (in English, for example, we can say 'ah' /ɑː/ if we make an interesting discovery, or 'sh' /ʃ/ if we want to call for quiet), but such cases are rare. The usual situation is for segments to fit closely together with each other. We have seen that phonetics tends to look on speech as a sequence of segments. However, to imagine these segments as discrete and independent of each other would be quite wrong. In every language we find that segments have a strong effect on other segments which are close to them. The process by which a segment is modified by its neighbours is called **assimilation**, and the description of assimilation has been a part of phonetic description for a long time. As we will see later, much recent phonetic research in this area refers to **coarticulation** instead, and we will discuss whether there is any significant difference between these terms. Another phenomenon of connected speech is **elision**, the process by which sounds that would be pronounced in slow, careful speech seem to disappear.

Assimilation

Let us look at some examples of assimilation. In French, a word-final voiceless consonant will often become voiced if followed by a voiced segment. For example, the word 'avec' on its own is pronounced /avek/, but when it is followed by a word beginning with a voiced consonant such as /v/ in 'vous' /vu/, we usually hear

/aveg/. So the phrase 'avec vous' is often pronounced /aveg vu/. In English, we also find assimilations of voice, but it is more common to find them in the form of *loss* of voice, or **devoicing**. If the word 'have' occurs in final position, its final consonant /v/ will usually have some voicing, but when that /v/ is followed by a voiceless consonant it normally becomes completely voiceless; thus 'I have to' is likely to have the pronunciation /aɪ hæf tu/.

Assimilation, then, is concerned with one sound becoming phonetically similar to an adjacent sound. The examples given so far are of anticipation, where a sound is influenced by the sound which follows it; another term frequently used for this type is *regressive* assimilation. We also find cases where the assimilation can be called *progressive*: here, not surprisingly, the process is for a sound to take on characteristics from a sound which precedes it. In general, this effect is less frequently found, though it is difficult to explain why this should be so. Historically, it must have been effective in English in order to produce the different pronunciations of the -s ending: the plural of 'cat' /kæt/ is 'cats' /kæts/ with a final /s/; the plural of 'dog' /dɒg/ is 'dogs' /dɒgz/ with /z/. The voicing of the suffix is conditioned by the voicing of the preceding final consonant.

Assimilations are traditionally classified into three main types, though as we shall see this classification is not completely adequate.

1 One type is assimilation of voice (we have seen examples of this taken from French and English); this may take the form of a voiced segment becoming voiceless as a consequence of being adjacent to a voiceless segment; alternatively, a voiceless segment may become voiced.

2 Another type is assimilation of place: this refers to changes in the place of articulation of a segment (usually a consonant). A well-known case is that of English word-final alveolar consonants such as /t, d, n/: if a word ending in one of these consonants is followed by a word whose initial consonant has a different place of articulation, the word-final alveolar consonant is likely to change so that it has the same place of articulation. Thus the word 'that' /ðæt/ may be followed by 'boy' /bɔɪ/ and become /ðæp/ (thus 'that boy' /ðæp bɔɪ/), or it may be followed by 'girl' and become /ðæk/ (thus 'that girl' /ðæk gɜːl/).

3 A third type is assimilation of manner: here one sound changes the manner of its articulation to become similar in manner to a neighbouring sound. Clear examples of this type are not easy to find; generally, they involve a change from a 'stronger' consonant (one making a more substantial obstruction to the flow of air) to a 'weaker' one, and are typical of rapid speech. An English example could be a rapid pronunciation of 'Get some of that soap', where instead of the expected /get sʌm əv ðæt səʊp/ the speaker says /ges sʌm ə ðæs səʊp/, with /s/ replacing /t/ in two words.

We should now consider what the reason is for these processes. We must remember that in most cases several articulators are involved in making a speech sound, and that they are not capable of moving instantaneously. In the example of French consonant voicing, the final consonant is intrinsically voiceless, but in the example given, it is preceded by a fully voiced vowel, and is followed by a voiced consonant. To produce a voiceless consonant usually requires the opening of the vocal folds to prevent voicing from happening. If the vocal folds are instead left in the position appropriate for the voicing of the vowel context, the result is likely to be that the consonant is produced with voicing, and we can suppose that this is why the consonant becomes voiced. This argument suggests that when we find assimilation, we can usually find an explanation based on what we know about how the relevant sounds are produced.

An important question arises at this point, which concerns the role of the phoneme in assimilation processes. Much of the earlier writing on assimilation has suggested that assimilatory changes generally involve a change from one phoneme to another; for example, the example 'I have to' is expressed as showing a change from /v/ to /f/; 'that girl' is supposed to show final /t/ changing to /k/ in /ðæk ɡɜːl/. Does this mean that all assimilations involve phonemic change of this sort? The answer must be 'no' — we can observe many cases in which there is a clear assimilation that does not involve phonemic change. An easy process to observe is the position of the lips. In a vowel such as English /iː/ (as in 'see'), the lips are spread, as for a smile. In a vowel such as English /ɔː/ (as in 'saw'), the lips are rounded and pushed forward. This spreading and rounding of the lips is quite a slow process, and it often happens that preceding and following sounds are also affected by it, even when they belong to a different word. Thus, the /s/ at the end of 'this' will tend to have spread lips in the phrase 'this evening' (where it precedes /iː/) and rounded lips in the phrase 'this autumn' (where it precedes /ɔː/). The effect is even more noticeable within a word: for example, the two /s/ sounds in 'see-saw', which precede /iː/ and /ɔː/ respectively, usually have very different lip-shapes. You can easily observe this effect in a mirror. The difference between rounded and non-rounded /s/ is not phonemic in English.

Can we always find an articulatory explanation for assimilation? These explanations seem to assume that we are basically lazy, and do as little work as possible—this is sometimes called the 'principle of least effort', and it does seem to explain a lot of human activity (or lack of it) in a very simple way. A good example is **nasalization**, particularly of vowels, and to understand this process we need to look at the activity of the **soft palate** or velum. When we produce a nasal consonant such as [m] or [n], the soft palate must be lowered to allow air to escape through the nasal cavity; however, for most vowels the velum is raised, preventing the escape of air by this route. In the English sentence 'I know' /aɪ nəʊ/ we would expect that if each segment were produced independently of its neighbours the soft palate would first rise for /aɪ/, then be lowered for /n/, then raised again for /əʊ/. But speech research has shown that the soft palate moves slowly and begins to make its movement some time before the completion of that movement is needed—in other words, we can see *anticipation* in its activity. As a result, the diphthong preceding [n] will be nasalized. We can see a more extreme example in a word like 'morning' /mɔːnɪŋ/ where all the vowels are next to nasal consonants, and the soft palate is often left in the lowered position for the whole word, producing nasalization of each of the vowels. In some languages, the difference between nasalized and non-nasalized vowels is phonemic, but this is not the case in English.

We have seen, then, that the picture of assimilation as a process which causes phonemic change is not adequate. The next point to make is that the simple idea of one sound influencing one neighbour is also unsatisfactory. Let us begin with an example where there is a regular process of a sound being changed only when it is *both* preceded *and* followed by an appropriate neighbour. In Tokyo Japanese, the vowels /i/ and /u/ regularly change into voiceless segments if they occur between voiceless consonants. Thus in the word 'futon' (the word for a type of bed), the /u/ vowel of the first syllable becomes a voiceless vowel, or simply a short burst of fricative noise, since the /u/ is preceded by the voiceless consonant /f/ and followed by the voiceless consonant /t/.

Coarticulation

The more deeply we look into the complexity of assimilatory processes, the more we need to move away from simple ideas like phoneme change and a single influencing neighbouring segment. This subject is of the most profound importance for understanding how speech is produced. If we want to follow recent experimental and theoretical work in this area that might help us to understand these processes, we must move on to the area of study known as **coarticulation**. In this field, the terms used in assimilation studies that were introduced above (*regressive* and *progressive*) are not usually used; it is more common to encounter the terms *anticipatory* and *perseverative* used (respectively) instead. Alternatively, terms which are easier to use but show a bias towards left-to-right alphabetic systems are *right-to-left* and *left-to-right*, respectively.

The name and the concept of coarticulation have been around since the 1930s, but it remains difficult to explain or define what coarticulation is. We have seen that traditional descriptions of assimilation appear to have concentrated on cases where a change of phoneme results from the assimilation process, or at least on cases where a clearly detectable change takes place which could be represented in phonetic transcription with a different symbol. We find a number of differences from this point of view when we study coarticulation, and I will begin by summarizing these briefly. First, the most important point is that we are interested in *all* aspects of the working together of different articulators, even if the result is difficult or impossible to detect by ear; this is because our primary interest in coarticulation phenomena is in finding a way to explain how the brain and the central nervous system control the muscles which move the articulators (the **neuromuscular** control of the articulators), rather than in describing the pronunciation of a particular language. Second, it has been demonstrated by many experimental studies that coarticulation has effects which extend much further than just from one segment to another, so coarticulation studies have to assume a more widely spread effect of segments on each other. Third, we take it to be a basic principle that coarticulation is something that can be explained in physical terms, and is not arbitrary. We will now look at these three characteristics of coarticulation in more detail.

When we talk about the brain controlling the production of speech, we make the assumption that there has to be a conversion from an *abstract* form of the utterance we are going to produce to a *physical* form that can be observed and measured. Part of the theoretical study of speech consists of making theories about what the abstract form might be like. In a very simple view, the brain would have the task of deciding what is to be said, and then assembling something resembling a phonemic transcription of it which would be stored somewhere in the brain. We know that the brain has a specific area which has the job of sending commands to the many muscles in the body, including those of the vocal tract, and it is therefore assumed that the instructions to produce each phoneme are passed to this area and converted into signals which cause the articulators to move and produce speech. While the instructions are being executed, various processes cause a partial merging together of the phonemes with the result that assimilation or coarticulation takes place. This view of the process has been likened by one writer to having a conveyor belt carrying eggs (the phonemes) passing between rollers which break the eggs and mix them together. The task of the brain is then to 'unscramble' the eggs and recognize each phoneme so that understanding of the message by the listener is possible. This picture of the speech production process is a very simple one, but while it is probably true to the facts to some extent, it is inadequate in so many ways that it must be drastically modified or rejected. The most important problem is that of time and timing: when we speak, our control of the time taken by each sound we make is very accurate. Yet we know that the task of synchronizing the movements of articulators is very complex: one problem is that the tracts of nerve fibres which carry the commands are of different lengths and work at different speeds. In the case of a consonant which involves a movement of the tongue tip and at the same time a movement of the vocal folds in the larynx to produce voicing, the impulses will reach the articulators in the mouth some time before they reach the larynx, yet the brain manages to arrange things in such a way that the commands all take effect at the right time. Another problem for the brain to deal with is the different mass of the various articulators: some articulators (for example, the tip of the tongue and the vocal folds) are light and mobile, while others (the tongue body, the soft palate) are relatively heavy and difficult to move quickly. Thus the problem of inertia has an effect on the timing and overlapping found in connected speech.

Coarticulatory effects often extend further than just from one sound to its neighbour. For example, in the word 'screws' /skru:z/, lip-rounding is often found extending over the whole word; it is actually required for the pronunciation of /u:/ and, for most English speakers, for the /r/ too, but it seems that the command to round the lips is sent to the articulators in time for the initial /s/ to be rounded, and this command will remain in effect after the end of the /u:/ so as to produce lip-rounding in the final /z/. This is not just an English characteristic: similar sound-sequences in French have been observed to form in the same way. The French word 'structural' contains two rounded /y/ vowels, and the lip-rounding may, again, be seen on the initial /s/ and through the word up to the beginning of the /a/ vowel. We have already seen how the vowels in the English word 'morning' /mɔ:nɪŋ/ will tend to be nasalized as a result of the lowering of the soft palate for the nasal consonants. All languages appear to exhibit some degree of coarticulatory nasalization of vowels adjacent to nasal consonants.

The third point is that, while studies of assimilation have tended to concentrate on clearly observable aspects of the pronunciation of a particular language, studies of coarticulatory processes are more likely to be looking for effects which are found (not necessarily in exactly the same form) in all languages because they are due to mechanical and biological limits on what the articulators can do in a given amount of time. To return to assimilation for a moment, we can observe in most accents of British English a rather surprising limit on regressive voicing assimilation. In the example 'I have to', given above, it was said that the /v/ is likely to lose any voicing it might have had, if it is followed by the voiceless consonant /t/. However, it is very unusual to find an English accent which permits regressive assimilation of voicing of the opposite type, that is, a final voiceless consonant becoming voiced as a result of being followed by a voiced consonant. Although this type of assimilation is common in many languages (see for example the French example given above of 'avec vous'), it is not found in English. The phrase 'nice voice' /naɪs vɔɪs/ will therefore not be pronounced with the /s/ changed to /z/, though French learners of English quite commonly do make this change and say /naɪz vɔɪs/, which sounds foreign to English ears. This effect is difficult to explain in terms of coarticulation. If we explain the French change of voiceless to voiced consonant in 'avec vous' as the result of the /k/ being influenced by the vocal fold activity of the neighbouring voiced consonants, how can we account for the fact that this does not happen in the case of English speakers, who are physically the same as the French speakers? The usual answer is said to lie in the difference between the phonetics and the phonology of a language: phonetically speaking, we are all built in much the same way and are subject to the same restrictions on what we can do in producing speech sounds. Phonologically speaking, however, each language has its own private set of rules, which makes it possible for each language to permit or prevent particular coarticulatory processes from taking place. In Spanish, the phonemes /b/, /d/, /g/ are normally pronounced as voiced plosives at the beginning of a word, but as voiced fricatives [β], [ð], [ɣ] between vowels. To Spanish speakers this seems a perfectly natural process which makes the phonemes in question more similar to vowels. In many other languages, this change from plosive to fricative does not happen at all. In others, it can be observed, but it is much less easy to detect. An example from English (BBC accent) would be the phrase 'getting better' /getɪŋ betə/, which in rapid speech is often pronounced with incomplete closure for the /t/ consonants. This results in weak fricatives being produced instead of plosives, though English speakers and listeners usually do not notice this; in the English spoken in southern Ireland, the effect is much more noticeable and is often detected by English people who know nothing about phonetics. There are thus language-specific, phonological constraints on how much coarticulation, and what type of coarticulation, will be found in a particular language.

Elision

To conclude this account of connected speech and coarticulation, we should look briefly at **elision**. Like assimilation, this is a topic which has had its place in the description of the pronunciation of languages for a very long time. The name refers to the disappearance of one or more sounds in connected speech which would be present in a word pronounced in isolation; the effect is also found when we compare rapid speech with slow, careful speech. If we take as an example the English sentence 'She looked particularly interesting', we could expect the pronunciation in slow, careful speech to be /ʃi lʊkt pətɪkjələli ɪntərəstɪŋ/ (which contains 27 phonemes); in rapid conversational speech, however, I might say /ʃi lʊk pətɪkli ɪntrstɪŋ/ (which contains 20). Where have the seven missing segments gone? The /t/ at the end of 'looked' has been left out because, we may assume, producing three voiceless plosives is hard work, and in English the middle one would not be pronounced audibly in any case. The other elisions are of syllables containing the 'schwa' vowel /ə/, which is so weak that it is usually one of the first items to disappear when speech is produced at higher speed. So the two syllables /jələ/ in 'particularly' are left out, as are the two schwa vowels before and after the /r/ in 'interesting'. As with assimilation, languages differ in which elisions, and how many, they allow, but all languages show some tendency in this direction. From the point of view of coarticulation studies, elision is not a separate process from assimilation. It is simply an extreme result of coarticulation whereby two sounds are articulated so closely in time to each other that a sound or sounds between them are completely obscured. The rapid speech version of 'looked particularly' in the above example is transcribed with no /t/ at the end of 'looked'; however, if we use laboratory instruments to observe what the tongue is doing, we often find that where it sounds as though a /t/ has disappeared, the tongue still makes a partial attempt to articulate a /t/, even though this is impossible to hear. Similarly, in the case of Japanese vowel devoicing, in rapid speech the vowel sometimes seems to disappear altogether; again, however, if we observe the contact between the tongue and the palate carefully, using laboratory instruments, we can see that the shape of the contact is different according to whether the missing vowel is (or was) /i/ or /u/. It would not be correct, therefore, to say that this is a case of a vowel phoneme being completely lost or deleted; it is more accurate to say that as a result of coarticulation, the neighbouring consonants have occupied all the time available and have overlapped on to the vowel.

There is a lot that we still do not understand about the changes that take place when we change from slow, careful speech to rapid, conversational speech. So much research is being carried out on this subject at the present time, however, that our knowledge is growing rapidly.

9
Variation

In traditional phonetic description, it has been usual to describe the characteristics of one particular type of speech. Where possible, analysts have looked for a 'standard' or 'model' accent. In Spain, for example, the accent of the region of Castilla (Castilian Spanish) has for centuries been treated as the 'purest' form of Spanish, and the one which foreigners should attempt to copy. In Britain, a similar standard traditionally known as **Received Pronunciation (RP)** was used for most of the twentieth century, though it is becoming more and more difficult to define what this is and to explain why it should be treated as special. As explained in Chapter 1, an increasing number of writers (myself included) now prefer to refer to the standard English pronunciation as a **BBC accent**. Perhaps the most common procedure in the past has been to adopt as a model the accent of educated people in the capital city of the country where the language is spoken. In some cases, however, descriptions are based simply on the pronunciation of speakers who were available to act as 'informants' to the analyst—this is frequently the case in studying languages spoken by only a few people, and which are likely to die out soon. In a few cases, a language has been recorded and analysed using the last surviving speaker of it, and the work done quickly because of the risk of the informant dying before the study was completed.

While this concentration on a single variety of a language is a convenient way of keeping one's description clear and simple, we should never forget that there is an enormous amount of variation in how a language is pronounced, and in this chapter we will look briefly at some of the types of variation.

Regional variation

The study of regional variation is probably the best-known and longest-established form of the study of variety, and most of us have a stereotyped picture of the earnest dialect researcher roaming through the countryside to seek out ancient rustic characters and elicit information about vocabulary and pronunciation. It is usual to make a distinction between the study of **dialect** (which looks not only at pronunciation but also vocabulary and grammar) and **accent** (which is purely a matter of pronunciation). We have already met the word 'accent' in a completely different use (to refer to distinctive pitch patterns), and this sometimes gives rise to confusions.

Regional variation can arise from many causes. One cause is invasion or colonization: parts of Britain, for example, were colonized by Norse and Saxon invaders while other parts remained unconquered, and there are still recognizable differences in English language and pronunciation due to this fact. Historically speaking, we can see that separate varieties were most likely to emerge when there were barriers and frontiers between the areas in which a language was spoken. Countries in which isolated communities have been separated from each other by mountains or sea often have greater differences in pronunciation than countries where there has been free and easy movement among people. We can see something of the sort on a very large scale in the way in which American English moved away from the pronunciation of English in England where it originated, thanks to the barrier of the Atlantic. When the first American 'talking' films were shown in Britain in the 1930s, the distributors had to consider putting subtitles on the films because most members of a British audience had virtually no experience of listening to an American accent. In the present day many people are able to communicate by phone with others who have very different varieties of the language, and can hear many different language accents on radio and television. Now spoken communication between British and American speakers seems relatively straightforward and misunderstandings are likely to be due to cultural differences rather than linguistic or phonetic ones.

There has been a recent growth of interest in a related area of the study of English pronunciation, sometimes referred to as English as an International Language. Since English is now used by so many people around the world for international communication, it is possible to see pronunciation varieties emerging which are not based primarily on the native-speaker accent of some part of the English-speaking world. Instead, they show English as a global 'common property' in which key phonetic and phonological distinctions are retained, but choosing to sound, for example, English or American seems irrelevant.

Social variation

To consider the complex ways in which social factors affect variation would take us into the domain of sociolinguistics and beyond the scope of the present book. But for our purposes we can broadly distinguish between three different kinds of variation. One is related to social class: in some societies (but certainly not in all) people have a pronunciation which identifies them as a member of some social class, or as being at some point on a scale from low to high social class. A good example is 'h-dropping': a well-known study in Bradford showed that speakers were more likely to pronounce the /h/ sound in words like 'house', 'hat', and so on if they were of higher social class, and more likely to omit it if they were of lower class.

A second type of social factor is speakers' tendency to use different pronunciations in different social situations. Not everyone does this, and many people who do it are reluctant to admit that they do. Many people can and do speak something like the standard accent in their professional life, but switch to a different accent (either a local regional variety or a lower-class pronunciation) when they are with family and friends.

Finally, there are social divisions in society other than class ones. Many languages show differences between the speech of men and women; different professional groups (for example, teachers or members of the armed forces) often have some distinctive accent or speaking style; and many societies, though with a common language, have strong differences of religion which are reflected in the variety of the language spoken.

Style variation

We are all capable of changing the way we speak when this is necessary for successful communication. Everyone can vary between speaking rapidly or slowly, or between quietly and loudly in a way that is appropriate to the communication situation (though some people make such adjustments more successfully than others). Phonetic descriptions of languages have tended to be made on the basis of a slow, careful speaking style, and this creates major problems when one comes to study more natural speech and discovers that it does not fit many of the 'facts' stated in textbook descriptions.

Teachers, priests, and politicians are good examples of people who need to be able to speak in a range of styles: public speaking is something which does not come easily to everyone, and in some cases people even take lessons in how to address a large group of people.

Age and variation

Everyone knows that young people speak differently from older people. It is not likely that this is due to physical causes. We do not know how much of age-based variation is due to individuals changing as they grow older and how much is due to the pronunciation changing from year to year. It is likely that a major factor is the wish of young people to speak in a different way from their parents, and in the present day this is strengthened by broadcasting aimed specially at young people. Some changes happen rapidly, while others emerge only over a very long period. Two changes in English have been specially noticeable since I began to work in phonetics in the mid-1960s. One is the growth in the use of the glottal stop (for which the phonetic symbol is [ʔ]), either as a replacement for the /t/ phoneme in words like 'getting', 'better' (so that 'getting better' is pronounced [geʔɪŋ beʔə]), or in conjunction with /p/, /t/, /k/, or /ʧ/ where the glottal closure precedes the oral closure in words like 'captive' [kæʔptɪv], 'cats' [kæʔts], 'accent' [æʔksənt], and 'butcher' [bʊʔʧə]. The other change is the fronting of the /uː/ vowel, most noticeably after /j/. In the early twentieth century, the 'Received Pronunciation' version of this vowel was back and rounded in all contexts, but in the speech of younger English people from the South-East this vowel in words like 'union' /juːnɪən/, 'human' /hjuːmən/, and 'usual' /juːʒuəl/ has become more of a front vowel (nearer to the /iː/ vowel), and it now has very little lip-rounding. The word 'used' in 'I used to' thus sounds almost like the word 'yeast'.

The pronunciation of a language, then, is liable to constant change, and at any time there are many varieties which are found in different places and situations.

Choosing the speech to study

Ideally, we would like to study speech which is as natural and as close to 'real life' as possible, but it is often very difficult to collect carefully controlled material for scientific analysis in an everyday context. In most of our daily life, for example, we are surrounded by a lot of extraneous noise which can make a recording difficult to study accurately, so it is often felt preferable to record speakers in a studio (usually within a speech laboratory). However, one of the common complaints about laboratory studies of speech is that speech recorded in this way does not sound natural. The use of what is often referred to as 'lab speech' has a number of disadvantages. Often, speakers have to read what they say (from a written text or from a computer screen), instead of speaking spontaneously. This can have serious effects: for example, a common mistake is to let the speaker see the end of the list of items that they are reading—intonation and speaking rate tend to change as one gets near the end of a list. In a long recording, fatigue is another problem—while some people can happily talk to their friends for hours, recording prepared material in a recording studio becomes very boring (and therefore tiring) after 20 or 30 minutes. Another problem is that speakers tend to be selected from the people who can be found near the laboratory, and are thus usually students or staff of a university; it is astonishing that experiments using such people are almost always described as using 'normal' speakers: in relation to the population as a whole, people who teach or study in universities and who volunteer to be recorded are *not* normal. Finally, everyone who knows that there is a microphone near them that is picking up what they say tends to speak more carefully than they would if they were speaking spontaneously. The well-known 'observer's paradox' is based on the fact that we want to know how people speak when we are not there, but we (or a recorder) have to be there in order to observe what is said. This has led to some researchers recording people secretly when they are talking naturally, thinking that they are speaking in private. This seems to me to be completely unethical, and I would never recommend doing it. How can natural speech then be recorded for us to study? One possibility is to develop interviewing skills, as the sociolinguist William Labov has done, to the point where after some time the speaker becomes relaxed and absorbed in what they are saying and forgets about the presence of the microphone. Another widely used way of eliciting fairly natural speech in studio conditions is to give two or more speakers a task to complete using only speech. A typical example is the 'maps task', where two people are given maps of the same area, but with information missing. The speakers cannot see each other's map, so they can only discover how to plan a journey by discovering through verbal interaction the information that is missing. In my own work, I have used the sort of puzzle that you sometimes see in magazines, where two pictures are printed which are identical apart from a number of very small differences. One picture is given to each speaker: they cannot see the other's picture, so they have to talk to each other to find out where the differences are. Often they become so absorbed in this task that it is difficult to stop them when enough speech has been recorded.

The most important point about this discussion is that we should never ignore the variation that we find in different speaking styles, and should always plan carefully in deciding how to record data that is going to be used for the scientific study of speech.

10
Conclusion

What you have read in this book should have made it clear that speech is a living, dynamic, and many-sided aspect of human activity. It would be quite wrong to conclude that we now understand everything about speech and the different forms it can take. The study of phonetics is a thriving subject: there are many phonetics journals regularly publishing new papers, both theoretical and applied, and new books are appearing all the time. The techniques available to us for studying speech with the help of signal processing by computer are rapidly becoming more powerful and more widely available, while possibly the most important development for many decades has been the growth in the use of the Internet for communicating and teaching about phonetics. Already there is a wealth of material freely available on the Internet on almost every aspect of phonetics, speech research, and pronunciation teaching. This is probably the most exciting time to be working in this field since the explosion of interest in phonetics around the end of the nineteenth and the early part of the twentieth century.

Readings

Chapter 1
The science of speech

Text 1

P. DENES and E. PINSON: *The Speech Chain* (2nd edn.).
W. H. Freeman 1993, pages 3-4

Speech, as we have seen, is a process of making sounds as a way of connecting the brain of the speaker with that of the hearer. This text describes how the process can be understood as a chain of events.

A convenient way of examining what happens during speech is to take the simple situation of two people talking to each other. For example, you, as the speaker, want to transmit information to another person, the listener. The first thing you have to do is arrange your thoughts, decide what you want to say and then put what you want to say into *linguistic form*. ... This process is associated with activity in the speaker's brain, and it is from the brain that appropriate instructions, in the form of impulses along the motor nerves, are sent to the muscles that activate the vocal organs—the lungs, the vocal cords, the tongue, and the lips. The nerve impulses set the vocal muscles into movement which, in turn, produce minute pressure changes in the surrounding air. We call these pressure changes a *sound wave*. Sound waves are often called *acoustic waves*, because acoustics is a branch of physics concerned with sound.

The movements of the vocal organs generate a speech sound wave that travels through the air between speaker and hearer.

Pressure changes at the ear activate the listener's hearing mechanism and produce nerve impulses that travel along the acoustic nerve to the listener's brain. In the listener's brain, a considerable amount of nerve activity is already taking place, and this activity is modified by the nerve impulses arriving from the ear. This modification of brain activity, in ways that are not yet fully understood, brings about recognition of the speaker's message. We see, therefore, that speech communication consists of a chain of events linking the speaker's brain with the listener's brain. We shall call this chain of events the *speech chain*.

▷ *Not everyone agrees that we arrange our thoughts and decide what we want to say before producing linguistic forms. Do you feel that you always do this when you speak?*

▷ *Describe how this communication 'chain' would be different if you were communicating with someone in a non-vocal way such as writing, or the sign language used by the deaf.*

Text 2

J. D. O'CONNOR: *Phonetics*. Penguin 1991, pages 17–18

This text makes the point that it is not enough for phonetics to provide a taxonomy or descriptive list of the sounds that occur in a particular language but it must also be concerned with how these sounds are actually put to distinctive use.

… phonetic study … may be applied impartially to the sounds of any and every language, and may be used to describe and classify, in one all-embracing scheme, the sound features of all known languages, from Arabic to Zulu. But the phonetician is by no means content to act only as a taxonomist, a describer and classifier of sounds. He is interested, finally, in the way in which sounds function in a particular language, how many or how few of all the sounds of language are utilized in that language, and what part they play in manifesting the meaningful distinctions of the language. Because one knows what a sound is—how it is produced, what its physical characteristics are and what effect it has on the ear—one does not therefore know what it *does*, and the same sound may have quite different tasks to perform in different languages. That is to say, the difference in sound between *d* and *th* is used in English to differentiate between one word and another; *then/den, lather/ladder, breathe/breed*. In Spanish this is not so; the difference between *d* and *th* can never be used to differentiate one word from another because *th* only occurs between vowels, as in *todo* ('all'), and at the end of a word, as in *verdad* ('truth'), whereas the sound *d* never occurs in these positions. So in Spanish the two sounds can never be 'opposed' to each other in the same place in a word, and therefore they can never be 'distinctive'.

▷ *How does the example from Spanish in this text relate to the comparison of English and French given in Chapter 1 (page 10)? Do they illustrate the same thing?*

▷ *The examples in the text are given in spelling and not phonetic symbols. Which symbols from the list for English in Chapter 1 (page 6) do you think would be appropriate for these examples?*

Chapter 2
Making speech sounds

It is difficult to define exactly what the terms vowel *and* consonant *mean. These two readings show different approaches to the question.*

Text 3
D. JONES: *An Outline of English Phonetics* (first published 1918; 9th edn.). Cambridge University Press 1975, pages 23–4

The difference between a vowel and a consonant would seem to be fairly obvious, but defining the essential distinction between them turns out to be a difficult thing to do. This text, written by the great pioneer of English phonetics Daniel Jones, gives a definition based strictly on the physical properties of the sounds.

Every speech-sound belongs to one or other of the main classes known as Vowels and Consonants.

A vowel (in normal speech) is defined as a voiced sound in forming which the air issues in a continuous stream through the pharynx and mouth, there being no obstruction and no narrowing such as would cause audible friction.

All other sounds (in normal speech) are called consonants.

Consonants therefore include (i) all sounds which are not voiced (e.g. p, s, ʃ), (ii) all sounds in the production of which the air has an impeded passage through the mouth (e.g. b, ɪ, rolled r), (iii) all sounds in the production of which the air does not pass through the mouth (e.g. m), (iv) all sounds in which there is audible friction (e.g. f, v, s, z, h).

The distinction between vowels and consonants is not an arbitrary physiological distinction. It is in reality a distinction based on acoustic considerations, namely on the *relative sonority* or *carrying power* of the various sounds. Some sounds are more sonorous than others, that is to say they carry better or can be heard at a greater distance, when pronounced with the same length, stress, and voice-pitch. Thus the sound ɑ pronounced in the normal manner can be heard at a much greater distance than the sound p or the sound f pronounced in the normal manner. It so happens that the sounds defined as vowels are on the whole more sonorous than any other speech-sounds (when pronounced in the normal manner); and that is the reason why these sounds are considered to form one of the two fundamental classes.

The relative sonority or carrying power of sounds depends on their inherent quality (tamber) and must be distinguished from the relative 'prominence' of sounds in a sequence; *prominence* depends on combinations of quality with length, stress and (in the case of voiced sounds) intonation. When length and stress (degree of push from the chest wall) are constant and the intonation is level, the sounds defined as vowels are more prominent than the sounds defined as consonants; 'open' vowels are mostly more prominent than 'close' vowels; voiced consonants are more prominent than voiceless consonants; l-sounds and voiced nasal consonants are more prominent than other voiced consonants. The voiceless consonants have very little prominence in comparison with the voiced sounds, and the differences in prominence between the various voiceless consonants may as a rule be considered as negligible for practical linguistic purposes. It must always be remembered, however, that *more sonorous* sounds may become *less prominent*, and therefore more consonant-like, by diminishing length or stress, and that sounds of relatively small sonority may be made prominent by increasing length or stress.

▷ *Is it practical to decide whether a sound is a vowel or a consonant according to its prominence, as Jones suggests? How would you compare sounds as different as* [m, s, u, v, ɑ, l]? *One way (if you have a tape-recorder, or other recording device, with a level meter) would be to see what level each of these sounds reaches when you say it.*

▷ *Jones claims that we need the two different notions of* sonority *and* prominence. *The vowel* [ɑː] *is very sonorous, but it is more prominent in the word 'parking' and less prominent in 'embarkation'; the consonant* [f] *has low sonority, but is more prominent when pronounced long in 'brief fire' than in the word 'briefing'. Try saying these examples and see if you agree.*

Text 4
A. C. GIMSON, revised by A. CRUTTENDEN: *Gimson's Pronunciation of English* (5th edn.). Edward Arnold 1994, pages 27–8

The difference between vowel and consonant is given a more modern definition in this text which distinguishes between the physical ('phonetic') characteristics of a sound (or segment) and the way it is used in a particular language (a 'phonological' definition).

Two types of meaning are associated with the terms 'vowel' and 'consonant'. Traditionally, consonants are those segments which, in a particular language, occur at the edges of syllables, while vowels are those which occur at the centre of syllables. So, in *red, wed, dead, lead, said,* the sounds represented by <r,w,d,l,s> are consonants, while in *beat, bit, bet, but, bought,* the sounds represented by <a,i,e,u,ough> are vowels. This reference to the functioning of sounds in syllables in a particular language is a phonological definition. But once any attempt is made to define what sorts of sounds generally occur in these different syllable-positions, then we are moving to a phonetic definition. This type of definition might define vowels as median (air must escape over the middle of the tongue, thus excluding sounds like [l]), oral (air must escape through the mouth, thus excluding nasals like [n]), frictionless (thus excluding fricatives like [s]), and continuant (thus excluding plosives like [p]); all sounds excluded from this definition would be consonants. But difficulties arise in English with this definition (and with others of this sort) because English /j,w,r/, which are consonants phonologically (functioning at the edges of syllables), are vowels phonetically. ... The reverse type of difficulty is encountered in words like *sudden* and *little*, where the final consonants /n/ and /l/ form syllables on their own and hence must be the centre of such syllables even though they are phonetically consonants, and even though /n/ and /l/ more frequently occur at the edges of syllables, as in *net* and *let*. ...

... consonants can be voiced or voiceless, and are most easily described wholly in articulatory terms, since we can generally feel the contacts and movements involved. Vowels, on the other hand, are voiced, and, depending as they do on subtle adjustments of the body of the tongue, are more easily described in terms of auditory relationships.

▷ *The concept of the syllable is central to the distinction between vowel and consonant in this text. In Text 3, however, no mention is made of the syllable at all. Can you explain why?*

▷ *'Vowels are voiced'—would a voiceless vowel therefore have to be classed as a consonant? Voiceless vowels are found in a number of languages.*

Chapter 3
Classifying speech sounds

Text 5
J. D. O'CONNOR: *Phonetics*. Penguin 1991, pages 126–7

The most important thing about a phoneme is that it is different from all the other phonemes of a language. One way of highlighting this is by picking out particular features which differentiate one phoneme from another, usually using the sort of phonetic features mentioned in Text 4.

In classifying sounds, ... as in classifying items in any other group, all we need to do is to mention those features by which they differ and leave it at that. If all I have to do is classify [s] and [d], without considering any other sounds, I need only mention one feature, for instance that [s] is fricative and [d] is not, or that [d] is a stop and [s] is not, or that [d] has voice in it and [s] has none. Any one of these features is sufficient to separate the two sounds and it is not necessary to quote all three. But if I have to classify [s], [d] and [t], one feature is no longer enough: [s] is a fricative but both [d] and [t] are not; [d] and [t] are both stops, whilst [s] is not; [d] has voice in it, but both [s] and [t] have none. So we need two features to classify them: presence or absence of voice and presence or absence of stop or friction. If we want classify the sounds of a particular dialect we shall need more than these two features; all the sounds of English will need more features again, and if we attempt to classify all sounds of all languages, still more features will be needed, since no single language makes use of all the possibilities of the human vocal tract.

But there is a certain economy in the use to which features of this kind are put in making distinctions of sound; we do not necessarily have to look for a new feature every time we have to separate one sound from another. To specify the difference between [t] and [d] in *too* and *do* we may select the feature of voicing, [t] being voiceless and [d] voiced. Then when we come to [p] versus [b] and to [k] versus [g] we find the same feature operating, [p] and [k] voiceless, [b] and [g] voiced. To separate all six, we need only add the three different places of articulation.

▷ *O'Connor is here explaining the idea of distinctive features. What features would you devise to specify the difference between the following groups of sounds?*

[i, e, a] versus [ɑ, o, u]; [b, d, g] versus [m, n, ŋ]; [f, v, p, b] versus [s, z, t, d].

▷ *If you know a language other than English, can you think of any sets of sounds in another language that require a feature that is not required for English, or of any English features that might not be needed for that language? For example, French needs to distinguish nasalized vowels from non-nasalized ones, but English doesn't; English has to distinguish long vowels from short vowels, but this is not needed in Spanish.*

Text 6

INTERNATIONAL PHONETIC ASSOCIATION:
The Handbook of the International Phonetic Association.
Cambridge University Press 1999, pages 28–9.

Sounds can be described as physical, phonetic events, or as distinctive phonemes. There are, therefore, different ways of transcribing them with symbols. This text sets out the IPA's principles for transcription. Terms such as 'phonemic', 'phonetic', 'allophonic', etc. are explained.

Broad and narrow transcriptions

A connected text represented in terms of phonemes is known as a 'phonemic transcription', or, almost equivalently, a 'broad transcription'. The term 'broad' sometimes carries the extra implication that, as far as possible, unmodified letters of the roman alphabet have been used. This restriction may facilitate printing, and might be considered particularly if a phonemic transcription is to form the basis of a writing system. Under this definition a transcription of English hideout as /haidaut/ would be broad, while /haɪdaʊt/ would not be because it introduces letter shapes to the symbol for the phoneme /aɪ/ and the phoneme /aʊ/ which are not absolutely necessary for the unambiguous representation of the phonemes of English, but which may be desirable to remind the reader of the phonetic realization of these phonemes. Frequently, though, 'broad' is used merely as a way of referring to transcriptions which are phonemic, regardless of the letter shapes used to represent the phonemes. Phonemic transcriptions are one type of 'systematic' transcription, meaning they require the phonological patterns or 'system' of a language to be known before they can be made.

The term narrow transcription most commonly implies a transcription which contains details of the realization of phonemes. There are two ways in which such a transcription may come about. If a transcription is made in circumstances where nothing can be assumed about the phonological system, it is necessary to include all phonetic details because it is not clear which phonetic properties will turn out to be important. The transcription would be made taking into account only the phonetic properties of speech. This type of narrow transcription, as might be made in the first stages of fieldwork, or when transcribing disordered speech, is sometimes called an impressionistic transcription or a general phonetic transcription. ...

The other kind of narrow transcription containing realizational information is termed allophonic. If the relevant phonological system is known, a transcription can be devised which includes any number of additional symbols to indicate the phonetic realizations of the phonemes, i.e. their allophones. An allophonic transcription is also known as a systematic narrow transcription.

▷ *Here are some examples of the use of transcription:*
  1 *Many dictionaries give information about pronunciation by giving the words in transcription. Which sort of transcription is used?*
  2 *Speech therapists sometimes find that they are dealing with someone who produces particular phonemes in an unusual way. What sort of transcription should they use to represent what they hear?*
  3 *Field-workers discover a language that has not been met before, and want to write down what they hear. What type of transcription is suitable?*

Chapter 4
Tone and tone languages

Text 7
K. L. PIKE: *Tone Languages*. University of Michigan Press 1948, pages vi–viii

We have seen how speech sounds are classified in phonetics. Since tones are clearly significant, we need to find a way of classifying them. In this text, taken from Pike's pioneering work, you can see that he chooses to treat tones as equivalent to phonemes, and uses the term toneme *to refer to a distinctive tone.*

The principles of phonemic analysis now in general use in the analysis of segmental phonemes are equally applicable, in theory, to the study of tonal phonemes. Various special practical problems arise, however, when an investigator attempts to apply these principles to pitch data. In order to solve such problems it is advisable to modify the phonemic procedures, and to amplify phonemic theory, with particular reference to tone.

The basic difficulty in discovering and transcribing the significant lexical pitch units lies in the relative nature of these pitches. The absolute pitch is not pertinent as such. Rather, the pitch of one syllable in contrast to pitches of neighboring syllables constitutes the essence of tonemic distinctions. The general pitch of the voice of a speaker may change from utterance to utterance or even in the midst of an utterance; in this way all pitches may, for example, be lowered so that the lowest pitches of the first utterance are higher than the highest pitches of the later utterance. Nevertheless, the tonemes, the significant pitch contrastive units, remain unchanged; the relative pitches are the same in each utterance. ...

... To the foreigner who wishes to speak the language it may appear to be a matter of indifference whether the pitch of a certain syllable is lowered slightly because the general pitch level of the voice has fluctuated or because, say, two high tonemes are not 'allowed' in sequence and, therefore, the second of them is mechanically lowered to a mid toneme. But ... incorrect interpretation gives an entirely erroneous structural picture by treating data that are actually phonemic as nonphonemic and data that really are part of the grammatical structure as mere phonetic variation.

▷ Text 6 introduced the difference between 'broad' or 'phonemic' transcription and 'narrow' or 'allophonic' transcription for speech sounds. Can you think of equivalent ways of transcribing Pike's 'tonemes' that could be devised to take account of the sort of pitch variation that he refers to?

▷ Would you expect there to be problems of communication between adults and children speaking a tone language? If not, why not?

Text 8
PETER LADEFOGED: *A Course in Phonetics* (4th edn.).
Harcourt 2001, page 235

This short text gives a useful example of the 'grammatical' use of tone (to signify such things as case, tense, number, or gender, or to stand for prepositions), which in the past has received less attention than the 'lexical' use (where the difference in tone simply identifies one word rather than another).

Tone languages make two slightly different uses of pitch within a word. In the examples given so far, differences in pitch have affected the lexical (dictionary) meaning of a word. But many, if not most, tone languages also use pitch differences to make changes in grammatical (morphological) meaning. Thus in Igbo the idea of possession—roughly the equivalent of 'of' in English—may be expressed by a high tone. This high tone appears, for example, in the phrase meaning 'the jaw of a monkey.' The word for 'jaw' is [àgbà] with two low tones. The word for 'monkey' is [èŋwè], also with two low tones. But the phrase 'the jaw of a monkey' is [àgbá èŋwè], with a high tone on the second syllable of the word for 'jaw.' Thus the English word 'of' can sometimes be represented simply as a high tone on a particular syllable in Igbo.

▷ *Imagine English having evolved into a tone language in which the plural form of nouns is indicated by high tone instead of adding '-s', while singular nouns have low tone. The word 'cat' is now ˌcat in the singular and ˉcat in the plural. How would you transcribe the following sentences?*
1 That cat has won more prizes than the other cats
2 Cakes are things that I like to eat
3 The boys bought toys, a book, some pens, and three hats.

Text 9

DAVID ABERCROMBIE: *Elements of General Phonetics.*
Edinburgh University Press 1967, pages 105–7

Those of us who do not speak a tone language may think of tone as an academic problem for phonetic description. Abercrombie looks at some of the interesting questions that arise when we think of meaning being conveyed by tone in everyday life.

Tone languages must inevitably present special problems if they are used in circumstances which interfere with speech melody. When, for example, people are talking in a whisper, they are talking without phonation. There is therefore no fundamental, and no pitch fluctuation. If a tone language is whispered, an essential part of the structure of its words will be removed. How, then, can a whispered tone language be understood? A number of experiments have been made in attempts to answer this question, but it is possible that the question does not really arise in many tone-language communities—whispering just does not seem to be used in them. The experiments have shown that some tone languages cannot be understood in a whisper except by skilful guessing from the context, though there are others which do seem to be comprehensible. However it is usually found that in these latter the pitch patterns are always accompanied either by rhythmic characteristics that are preserved in whisper, or by register differences that can be simulated, and these in themselves are sufficiently distinctive to provide intelligibility.

Singing might seem to be another problem. Since a song imposes its own pitch pattern on the words that go with it, there is obviously the possibility of conflict if these words are words of a tone-language. When songs are imported from other cultures into a tone-language community—translations of hymns introduced by Christian missionaries, for example—the tunes may lead the singers to express sentiments different from those intended. Indigenous song, however, seems always to be accommodated to speech melody patterns so that ambiguities do not result.

But if tone languages seem to entail problems in communication from which intonation languages are free, they also have advantages which intonation languages do not possess. We saw from the case of whisper that, in a tone language, segments—vowels and consonants—without speech melody have little intelligibility. The converse, rather unexpectedly, is not the case. If the segments are removed, leaving only the speech melody, the words of a tone language preserve considerable intelligibility. But once the speech melody is divorced from the vowels and consonants, it no longer needs a human voice to convey it: any means of producing notes of varying pitch can do so, and there are many means which have more carrying power than the human voice. This is the secret of the talking drums in Africa. Drum signalling is not by means of a code: the signals are a direct transfer of linguistic pitch patterns and rhythmic patterns to the drums. The advantages of this for long distance communication are obvious. Various other instruments are used in some tone-language communities for conveying the pitch patterns of words—flutes or horns, for instance.

▷ *If you speak a tone language, do you think you can whisper your language intelligibly? If your language is a non-tone language, do you think you can convey pitch differences corresponding to 'yes' (normal agreement), 'yes?' (question), and 'yes!' (emphatic)?*

▷ *Even people who do not speak a tone language use pitch in lots of 'non-linguistic' sounds that they produce in everyday conversation—English speakers use different pitch on 'mm' a lot, for example. Can you think of the pitch you might use to indicate agreement, questioning, and expressing doubt? Do you have a regular pitch movement for expressing disgust, with a syllable like 'ugh'?*

Chapter 5
Suprasegmentals

The previous chapter showed how the tones of tone languages can be analysed, despite the considerable practical and theoretical difficulties involved. The analysis of suprasegmental features of languages which do not have contrastive tone presents different but equally difficult problems.

Text 10
ALAN CRUTTENDEN: *Intonation* (2nd edn.). Cambridge University Press 1997, pp. 14–15.

One of the most important areas of suprasegmental phonology is stress (sometimes called 'accent'). This text explains the different ways in which stress is used in various languages.

Many languages have word-stress regularly in a certain position on almost all words: Czech and Finnish typically have the stress on the first syllable; Spanish and Welsh typically on the penultimate syllable; and French and Turkish typically on the final syllable. Compare, for example:

Finnish— týtar 'daughter'; líkainen 'dirty'; mérimies 'sailor'.
Spanish— bastánte 'enough'; mañána 'tomorrow';
    múchos 'many'.
French— compagníe 'company'; bagáges 'luggage'; maláde 'ill'.

The stress marks on the above words are not, of course, included in the ordinary orthography of these languages. Nor do the examples given tell the whole story for the languages concerned. In Spanish most words end in a vowel and such words do have penultimate stress as stated; but words ending in a consonant more usually have final stress, e.g. *tomár* 'take'. In addition there are a number of absolute exceptions like *próximo* 'next' (in these cases Spanish orthography does actually mark the stress). Most languages with so-called 'fixed' word-stress are not usually as simple as that term implies; nevertheless it is true that word-stress is at least fairly easily predictable in such languages. Because it is predictable stress takes on a strong DELIMITATIVE FUNCTION in such languages. If I know that words generally begin with a stressed syllable in Finnish, my ear will easily segment the stream of speech into words. However, once again, the real situation is often not quite as simple as this. While French words, for example, regularly have their stress on the final syllable, many words will lose their stress in connected speech and hence stress will only occur at the end of a group of words, e.g.

Les múrs de votre maisón sont trop nóirs

Hence the occurrence of an accent delimits a word group rather than a single word in French.

  Other languages hardly use word-stress in a delimitative way at all. In particular, this is true of languages like English which have little predictability in their word-stress. ...

  There are, then, languages which do not use word-stress delimitatively and use it distinctively only to a very restricted extent. In such languages word-stress may be in part predictable but only by a set of complex rules. Such a language is English and a great deal has been written about the rules necessary to predict word-stress in English.

▷ *As mentioned in Chapter 5 of the Survey (page 32) there are
 some pairs of words in English which differ only in their*

*stress patterns. Can you produce a simple rule that accounts
for stress placement in all the following examples? (Stress is
here indicated by the mark ').*

1 'abstract (adjective); ab'stract (verb)
2 'insult (noun); in'sult (verb)
3 'perfect (adjective); per'fect (verb)
4 'record (noun); re'cord (verb).

▷ *What happens to your rule when it is confronted with words
such as 'audit', 'measure', 'blanket', which can be both nouns
and verbs? Can you find a solution to the problem?*

Text 11

JOHN CLARK and COLIN YALLOP: *An Introduction to
Phonetics and Phonology* (2nd edn.). Blackwell 1995,
page 358.

*The important point made in this text is that some aspects of
suprasegmental phonology must be regarded as centrally important aspects of language, not as some added-on emotional
colouring of what we say.*

The importance of English intonation, both as an area of difficulty
for the foreign learner and as a challenge to theory and description, has been acknowledged in a number of classic studies. ...

Intonation is often described, somewhat impressionistically,
as a matter of 'musical features' or speech 'tunes or melodies' ... .
While this may be a useful nontechnical pointer, it is sometimes
linked with a conception of intonation as something superimposed
upon the intrinsic meaning of words themselves, conveying the
speaker's attitude rather than any fundamental meaning ... . It is
true that the prosodic features of utterances—including such
aspects as tempo and overall pitch setting—signal what may
loosely be summarized as 'attitudinal' factors, such as the speaker's anger or tiredness. It would nevertheless be an injustice to
English intonation to suggest that it does no more than provide
an overlay of feelings or emotions. It is in fact a crucial part of the
English language, carrying important semantic functions. These
functions may be 'attitudinal' in the sense that they express, for
instance, definiteness or tentativeness, but these meanings are no
more superimposed or extrinsic than other functional options such

as whether to ask a question or make a statement or whether to qualify a statement by including the word 'probably' or 'possibly'.

If we narrow the concept of intonation to exclude both basic rhythm ... and overall settings (such as faster or slower rate of utterance and higher or lower pitch range), there remain three functional ingredients that are central to English intonation: TONE, or pitch pattern, TONE PLACEMENT ('sentence stress' ...) and TONE GROUP STRUCTURE.

▷ *Why do you think the authors suggest excluding rhythm and 'overall settings' from the analysis of intonation?*

▷ *The authors include 'sentence stress' (the placement of the strongest stress on a particular word in a sentence) as a part of intonation. What differences in meaning can you make by changing sentence stress?*

Text 12

HEINZ GIEGERICH: *English Phonology*. Cambridge University Press 1992, pages 258–9

The rhythm of spoken language is a controversial area of study. This text questions the clear-cut distinction that used to be made between 'stress-timed' and 'syllable-timed' languages.

... it has been claimed that languages are either syllable-timed or stress-timed, where French and Italian, for example, are said to belong in the former group and English, German and Russian in the latter. ...

But such a strictly dichotomous classification of the languages of the world is misleading in two respects. Firstly, there are languages that show signs of both syllable-timing and stress-timing: in Spanish, for example, both syllables and stresses recur at intervals that appear to be rhythmically structured. The distinction between syllable-timed and stress-timed languages, then, is not dichotomous but scalar. ... Secondly, in the long history of experimental measurements of foot durations in English, it has not been unequivocally shown that foot isochrony 'exists' on the production side of speech: rather, the question remains highly controversial.

> We can see very marked stress-timing in English children's nursery rhymes. Do you think that there is any similarity between this rhythm and the rhythm of conversational English?

> If you were able to measure the lengths (durations) of syllables, how might you construct a test to decide if a language were stress-timed or syllable-timed?

Chapter 6
Acoustics of speech sounds

Text 13

R. D. KENT, J. DEMBOWSKI, and N. J. LASS: 'The acoustic characteristics of American English' in N.J. Lass (ed.): *Principles of Experimental Phonetics*. Mosby 1996, page 187

This text summarizes the basic concept of the source-filter theory of speech acoustics. It shows that vowels provide the clearest examples for this theory, but it can also be used in the study of obstruents (sounds like plosives and fricatives), nasals, glides (such as [j] and [w]), and liquids (such as [l] and English [ɹ]).

The acoustic theory of speech production posits that the vocal tract sound production system may be decomposed into two primary components: a source, which provides the input to the system, and a filter, which modulates the input. Thus, the acoustic theory is alternatively known as the source-filter theory. ... Speech production involves three primary sound sources: (1) a ... periodic laryngeal voicing source, typified in the phonation of vowels, (2) a transient aperiodic noise source, exemplified by the release burst of stop consonants, and (3) a continuous aperiodic turbulent (noise) source used in the production of fricatives. Alone or in combination, these sources provide the vocal tract input for the sounds that make up the phonetic system of English and many other languages as well. Source-filter theory may be applied to any of the phonetic segments of English, but it is most often presented, and perhaps most easily understood, as a way of conceptualizing vowel production. It may be generalized to obstruents, nasals, glides, and liquids.

▷ *Vowels are normally produced with voicing as the source and the vocal tract acts as a filter to impose the characteristics of a particular vowel. What is different when you whisper a vowel?*

▷ *The above text makes no mention of the aspiration noise. What is the primary source for aspiration, and what filtering effect would you expect to find?*

Text 14

R. J. BAKEN: *Clinical Measurement of Speech and Voice.* Taylor and Francis 1987, page 353

Although we can make precise measurements of acoustic characteristics of a particular sound, we should not forget that the brain is constantly having to adjust to different speakers, calculating differences in relative terms. In the case of vowels, this makes it necessary to look at differences in the frequencies of formants, the characteristic peaks of energy at different frequencies.

The formant pattern of a vocalic sound (and in particular the relationship of its first two formants) is crucial to its perceptual categorization by a listener ... . However, formant frequencies do not necessarily uniquely specify the vowel that is perceived. ... Identification is influenced by the listener's linguistic experience, speaker fundamental frequency, the vowel's phonetic context, stress or prominence, and formant amplitude ... .

Since formants reflect the size and shape of the vocal tract, there is no reason to expect that absolute formant frequencies should remain constant in the face of anatomical variation among speakers. What are important are the relative frequencies of the formant peaks, their positions with respect to each other and to the formants of other vowels produced by the same speaker ... . However, even the relativity of formant frequencies may not be perfectly preserved across speakers. If it were, one would expect that, for a given vowel, the ratio of the frequencies of the first and second formants would remain stable across men and women, and across older and younger children, whose vocal tracts are all different in size and shape. There are indeed linear trends in inter-personal formant scaling, but the exact relationships are neither simple nor perfectly understood. ...

▷ In Text 7 you read about the problem of recognizing tones when each individual speaks with a different pitch range. In what ways is the problem of recognizing different speakers' vowels by their formant frequencies, referred to in the present text, similar?

▷ The 'interpersonal formant scaling' referred to by Baken would result in our being able to use a mathematical formula to remove the differences between the formant frequencies of women, men, and children, and some people hope that this will enable computers to recognize the speech of a wide range of people. The text suggests some reasons why this transformation would not solve all the problems of interpersonal variation. What are the remaining problems?

Chapter 7
Sounds in systems

The first two texts discuss the segments that are found in languages around the world, and you will see that there are substantial differences.

Text 15
IAN MADDIESON: *Patterns of Sounds*. Cambridge University Press 1984, pages 7–8.

The research discussed in this text involves the use of a database which lists information about segmental phonemes in a large number of the world's languages. This database makes it possible to describe general trends in the way languages have patterns of sounds.

The number of segments in a language may vary widely. The smallest inventories included in the survey have only 11 segments (Rotokas, Mura) and the largest has 141 (!Xū). However, it is clear that the typical size of an inventory lies between 20 and 37 segments—70% of the languages in the survey fall within these limits. The mean number of segments per language is a little over 31; the median falls between 28 and 29. ...

Whether the tendency to have from 20 to 37 segments means that this is an optimum range is an open question. It seems likely that there is an upper limit on the number of segments which can be efficiently distinguished in speech, and a lower limit set by the minimum number of segments required to build an adequate vocabulary of distinct morphemes. But these limits would appear to lie above and below the numbers 37 and 20 respectively .

Consider the following: the Khoisan language !Xũ with 141 segments is related to languages which also have unusually large inventories. Comparative study of these languages indicates that large inventories have been a stable feature which has persisted for a long time in the Khoisan family. If the number of efficiently distinguished segments was substantially smaller, there would be constant pressure to reduce the number of segments. There does not seem to be any evidence of such pressure.

Similarly, the facts do not seem to show that languages with small inventories (under 20 segments) suffer from problems due to lack of contrastive possibilities at the morphemic level. The symptoms of such difficulties would include unacceptably high incidence of homophony or unmanageably long morphemes. Dictionaries and vocabularies of several languages with small inventories do not provide evidence that there are symptoms of stress of these kinds in languages with small phoneme inventories. Hawaiian, for example, with 13 segments has been calculated to have an average of just 3.5 phonemes per morpheme, clearly not unacceptably long. And again, comparative evidence indicates that small inventory size may be a phenomenon which persists over time, as, for example, in the Polynesian language family, which includes Hawaiian.

▷ *Counting the number of contrasting segments in a language is not always as straightforward as the above text seems to suggest. How does the segment inventory of English cast doubt on the reliability of the figures quoted for other languages?*

▷ *Would you expect it to be easier to learn the pronunciation of a language with a smaller number of segments than that of your own language?*

Text 16

DAVID ABERCROMBIE: *Elements of General Phonetics.*
Edinburgh University Press 1967, pages 82–3

There is a risk, in looking at the inventories of segments in different languages, of overlooking the importance of the contrasts that exist among the segments in a phonological system. This text emphasizes this point.

The other concept used for describing the phonology of a language ... is the concept of system. A system is an inventory of the items in a language that can represent one of the two elements of structure, C or V; there is thus a C-system and V-system. The two are often referred to together as the sound-system of a language. Languages can differ from each other in the matter of system, as well as in structure.

An immediately obvious difference between languages is in the size of their systems, that is to say in the number of items they contain. V-systems, for instance, may range from three items, as in Classical Arabic and some modern forms, through five (modern Greek, Spanish), seven (Italian), eight (Turkish), to much larger systems such as those used by educated speakers in Britain, which may comprise from thirteen to twenty-one items. C-systems, also, may be small (but never, as far as is known, as small as V-systems can be): Hawaiian has eight, English twenty-two, Scots Gaelic about thirty, some American Indian languages, such as Tlingit, spoken in Alaska, over forty.

There seems to be no necessary relation between the size of the V-system of a language and the size of its C-system; both may be large, or both small, or one small and the other large. An extreme example of the latter case is provided by Kabardian, a Caucasian language, which has forty-five items in its C-system, and three in the V-system.

▷ *In addition to studying the segments of different languages, phonologists are also interested in how the C and V elements that Abercrombie refers to combine together into syllables. How many consonants can occur at the beginning and at the end of an English syllable? Compare this with any other language that you know.*

▷ *If it is useful to distinguish between systems of consonants and vowels, would it also be useful to distinguish between systems of different types of consonants and of vowels?*

Text 17

LARRY HYMAN: *Phonology: Theory and Analysis.* Holt, Rinehart and Winston 1975, pages 16–17

Much has been learned about the speech sounds made by adults. Another very interesting area is the study of how children acquire the sound system of their language.

We ... owe to Jakobson ... the observation that, in all languages, sound segments tend to be learned in a relatively fixed order by children. While more recent studies have not always confirmed the details of Jakobson's relative chronology of sound acquisition, certain general tendencies cannot be missed. It can be observed, for instance, that children learning English acquire [f] before they acquire [θ]. A child is quite likely to produce a word such as *thumb* with an initial [f]. As a result, the word *three* may become homophonous with the word *free*. Other general tendencies include the learning of voiceless stops before voiced stops, as well as the learning of front consonants such as [p] and [t] before back consonants such as [k]. This last tendency is revealed by the predominance of front consonants in the following common forms for 'mother' and 'father' in child language ... :

LABIAL		DENTAL/ALVEOLAR	
nasal	mama	nana	'mother'
oral	papa/baba	tata/dada	'father'

The presence of labial or dental/alveolar consonants in the forms for 'mother' and 'father' is widely attested in the acquisition of unrelated languages. In addition, cross-linguistic investigations of child language indicate a nasal consonant in 'mother' but an oral consonant in 'father.' While the above forms are frequently heard, it is rarely the case that a child refers to his mother as [ŋaŋa] and to his father as [kaka]. The statistical bias in favor of front consonants in the terms 'mother' and 'father' is presumably due to the fact that labial and dental/alveolar consonants are learned before velar consonants. Thus, numerous studies in child language have reported children replacing velars by dental/alveolar consonants.

▷ *Think of the words for 'mother' and 'father' in all the languages you know and see if they follow regular patterns as predicted above. How much difference is there between children's words for parents ('mummy', 'daddy') and those used by adults ('mother', 'father')?*

▷ *Might there be a physiological reason for the child's word for 'mother' containing a nasal consonant while that for 'father' tends to be non-nasal?*

Chapter 8
Connected speech and coarticulation

Text 18
A. C. GIMSON, revised by A. CRUTTENDEN: *Gimson's Pronunciation of English* (5th edn.). Edward Arnold 1994, pages 254–5.

Gimson presents an account of assimilation from the point of view of traditional descriptive phonetics.

We have seen ... that our basic linguistic units, the phonemes, represent abstractions from actual phonetic reality. If the phoneme /t/ is given a convenient, generalised label—a voiceless alveolar plosive—it is nevertheless true that the actual phonetic realisation of this consonant depends on the nature of the context, e.g. /t/ is aspirated when before a vowel (except after /s/), and dental, rather than alveolar, when adjacent to /θ/ or /ð/. Phonetically, we are dealing with a sound and articulatory continuum rather than with discrete units: features of sound segment A may be found in the following segment B, and features of B in A ... . If, therefore, the utterance is analysed in terms of a sequence of phonemes, account must be taken of the phonetic continuity and merging of qualities by describing the mutual influence which contiguous elements exert upon each other; in other words, tendencies towards assimilation or *coarticulation* have to be noted. ...

Variations of articulation may be of an allophonic kind, either within a word or at word boundaries; or, at word and morpheme boundaries, they may be of such an extent that a change of phoneme is involved, as between the pronunciation of a word in isolation and that which it may have in context. The fact that the phonemic pattern of a word is subject to variation emphasises the potential nature of phonemic oppositions. ... The mutual influence of contiguous phonemes in English functions predominantly in a *regressive* or *anticipatory* direction, i.e. features of one phoneme are anticipated in the articulation of the preceding phoneme; sometimes it is *progressive* or *perseverative*, i.e. one phoneme markedly influences the following phoneme; and sometimes it is coalescent, i.e. a fusion of forms takes place.

▷ *In this account of assimilation, how much importance is given to the phoneme? What is meant by 'variations of articulation ... of an allophonic kind'?*

▷ *This text says that phonemes 'represent abstractions from actual phonetic reality'. What does it mean to say that they are abstractions?*

Text 19

EDDA FARNETANI: 'Coarticulation and connected speech processes' in W. J. Hardcastle and J. Laver (eds.): *The Handbook of Phonetic Sciences*. Blackwell 1997, pages 371–404 (extracts taken from pages 371–9)

Farnetani is writing in the context of laboratory studies of coarticulation, and looks at the possible difference between assimilation and coarticulation.

During speech the movements of different articulators for the production of successive phonetic segments overlap in time and interact with one another. As a consequence, the vocal tract configuration at any point in time is influenced by more than one segment. This is what the term 'coarticulation' describes. The acoustic effects of coarticulation can be observed with spectrographic analysis: any acoustic interval, auditorily defined as a phonetic segment, will show the influence of neighbouring phones in various forms and degrees. Coarticulation may or may not be audible in terms of modifications of the phonetic quality of a segment. This explains why descriptive and theoretical accounts of coarticulation in various languages became possible only after physiological and acoustical methods of speech analysis became available and widespread, that is, during the last thirty years. ...

Assimilation refers to contextual variability of speech sounds, by which one or more of their phonetic properties are modified and become similar to those of the adjacent segments. We may ask whether assimilation and coarticulation refer to qualitatively different processes, or to similar processes described in different terms (the former reflecting an auditory approach to phonetic analysis, and the latter an instrumental articulatory/acoustic approach). ...

Current theories of coarticulation offer controversial views on whether there are qualitative or quantitative or even no differences between assimilatory and coarticulatory processes.

▷ *Farnetani takes a neutral view on whether the terms 'assimilation' and 'coarticulation' refer to the same thing. What differences can you point to which might resolve this question?*

▷ *'... the vocal tract configuration at any point in time is influenced by more than one segment'. Is this true without exception?*

Chapter 9
Variation

Text 20
PETER TRUDGILL: *The Dialects of England* (2nd edn.). Blackwell 1999, page 3

In an interesting and simple book, Trudgill explains with some examples the importance of the distinction between dialect *and* accent.

If you speak Lancashire dialect, you will obviously speak it with a Lancashire accent. But it is worth making a distinction between accent and dialect because of what happens with the important dialect we call Standard English. Standard English is the dialect which is normally used in writing, and which is spoken by the most educated and powerful members of the population: probably no more than 12–15 per cent of the population of England are native speakers of Standard English.

The fact is that everybody who speaks with a BBC accent also speaks the Standard English dialect ... . But not everybody who speaks Standard English does so with a BBC accent. Most people who speak Standard English ... do so with some kind of regional accent ... . This accent and this dialect do not therefore inevitably go together, and it is useful to be able to distinguish, by using the terms dialect and accent, between speakers who combine them and those who do not.

▷ *Try to decide, in relation to your own language, whether you speak the standard variety (dialect and accent) of your language, or a different one. If you find this difficult (many people do), could this be because the notion of 'standard language' is not as simple as it seems?*

▷ *Why do you think people hold such strong views about dialects and accents?*

Text 21

PAUL FOULKES and GERARD DOCHERTY: *Urban Voices.* Edward Arnold 1999, pages 11–12

Surveying contemporary research themes in accent studies, the authors comment on the status of a standard accent.

Several recent studies have in fact shown indications that non-standard varieties are coming to exercise more and more influence on variation and change. ...

The emergence of influential non-standard varieties raises important issues concerning the ongoing status of the standard as a reference point for speakers, the social and geographical networks which facilitate influence and contact between varieties, and the nature of the contact which is required for influence to take place. What is certainly clear is that we can no longer assume that speakers of non-standard varieties automatically orient themselves towards the standard: variation and ongoing change may potentially be influenced by a range of external varieties. Given the changing status of RP, we might perhaps reassess the continuing role of RP as an educational norm, particularly with regard to the teaching of English as a foreign language.

The standard variety furthermore plays a prominent role in most descriptive dialectological work. However, this too is not without its drawbacks. When describing a regional accent or non-standard dialect, it is usual to refer to the standard form, at least implicitly, to enable readers unfamiliar with the variety being described to understand its features.

▷ *You will have noticed, in the earlier part of this book, doubts about the value of RP as the ideal version of British English for foreign learners to aim at. So what should be our 'educational norm', and why?*

▷ *If you were a visitor from another planet trying to analyse the language and speech of people on Earth, would you find it necessary to identify the standard language and the standard accent of the language you were studying before you could start describing the different varieties of that language?*

SECTION 3

References

The references which follow can be classified into introductory level (marked ■□□), more advanced and consequently more technical (marked ■■□), and specialized, very demanding (marked ■■■).

Chapter 1
The science of speech

■□□

VIVIAN COOK: *Inside Language*. Arnold 1997

Chapter 4 ('The sound system of language') gives a simple introduction to phonetics and phonology, and looks ahead to a number of topics that are introduced in later chapters of the present book.

■□□

P. B. DENES and E. PINSON: *The Speech Chain* (2nd edn.). W. H. Freeman 1993

The book as a whole contains much useful reading to supplement several chapters in the present book, though readers may find some of the details of the physics, anatomy, and physiology of speech difficult. The examples are based on American English. Chapters 1 and 2 make good, simple introductory reading, while Chapters 3 to 7 are worth reading to supplement later chapters. Chapters 9 to 11 lead you into territory (digital speech processing and speech technology) that cannot be covered in the present book.

Chapter 2
Making speech sounds

■□□

PETER ROACH: *English Phonetics and Phonology* (3rd edn.). Cambridge University Press 2000

Chapters 2, 3, and 4 of this introductory book give a brief outline of such matters as the difference between vowels and consonants, the production of the airflow in speech, voicing, and some major classes of speech sound.

■□□

PETER LADEFOGED: *A Course in Phonetics* (4th edn.). Harcourt 2001

The whole of this book makes a good introduction to phonetics, but Chapters 1 and 6 are particularly useful in the context of this chapter.

■■□

JOHN CLARK and COLIN YALLOP: *An Introduction to Phonetics and Phonology* (2nd edn.). Blackwell 1995

Chapters 2 and 3 of this book give a clear and detailed account of sound production. Some of this material is also relevant to the topic of Chapter 3 of this book. Chapter 6 gives a thorough and detailed account of the anatomy and physiology of speech production.

Chapter 3
Classifying speech sounds

■□□

INTERNATIONAL PHONETIC ASSOCIATION: *The Handbook of the International Phonetic Association*. Cambridge University Press 1999

This is the official account of the IPA's categorization of speech sounds and use of phonetic symbols, and is a very valuable book for students of phonetics.

■■□

PETER LADEFOGED and IAN MADDIESON: *The Sounds of the World's Languages*. Blackwell 1996

This account contains a large amount of information about the enormous range of sounds used contrastively in the world's languages; in their field work over many years, the writers have themselves often been the first to describe them in detail.

■■□

JOHN LAVER: *Principles of Phonetics*. Cambridge University Press 1994

In Parts II, III, and IV of this very substantial book (pages 95–335), Laver sets out a detailed and comprehensive account of how the sounds of speech can be unambiguously categorized, with a wealth of illustrations from different languages.

Chapter 4
Tone and tone languages

■□□

PETER LADEFOGED: *A Course in Phonetics* (4th edn.). Harcourt 2001

The linguistic use of pitch, with particular reference to tone languages, is set out in pages 233–40.

■■□

FRANCIS KATAMBA: *An Introduction to Phonology*. Longman 1989

Katamba's book, on pages 186–208, presents a clear introduction to the nature of tone and the way in which modern phonology tries to deal with the problems it presents.

■■□

JOHN LAVER: *Principles of Phonetics*. Cambridge University Press 1994

Section 15.6 (pages 462–83) of Laver's book contains a wide-ranging survey of the phonetics of tone in tone languages.

Chapter 5
Suprasegmentals

■□□

ALAN CRUTTENDEN: *Intonation* (2nd edn.). Cambridge
University Press 1997

An excellent introduction to the study of intonation, this book
also gives good coverage of other suprasegmental features such
as stress, accent, and rhythm. It is mainly based on English.

■■□

D. ROBERT LADD: *Intonational Phonology*. Cambridge
University Press 1996

Although difficult in places, Chapter 1 of this important book is a
very good survey of some of the key questions in contemporary
thinking on intonation. Ladd attempts a definition of intonation,
a justification of its phonological status, and an evaluation of laboratory studies. He excludes 'lexical' features (properties of words
such as word-stress patterns), and proposes that intonation instead conveys 'post-lexical' pragmatic meanings in a linguistically
structured way. Section 1.2 of this chapter looks at one particular
theory of intonation (the IPO approach), but it is not necessary to
read this to understand the principal points of Ladd's treatment.

■■□

DANIEL HIRST and ALBERT DI CRISTO (eds.): *Intonation
Systems*. Cambridge University Press 1998

The intonation of twenty languages is presented in this collection
by specialists in those languages. Although the editors did not
succeed in persuading all the authors to use the same descriptive
system, the material does allow useful comparisons between different languages to be made.

Chapter 6
Acoustics of speech sounds

■□□
MARTIN BALL and JOAN RAHILLY: *Phonetics: The Science of Speech*. Edward Arnold 1999

Chapter 9 introduces fundamental concepts of acoustics and their application to the study of speech.

■□□
PETER LADEFOGED: *Vowels and Consonants*. Blackwell 2001

In this book, the sounds of speech are described both in the traditional way and also in terms of their acoustic characteristics.

■■□
KEITH JOHNSON: *Acoustic and Auditory Phonetics*. Blackwell 1997

This is a comprehensive introduction to speech acoustics. It does, of course, go considerably further than the basic coverage of Chapter 6.

Chapter 7
Sounds in systems

■□□
A.C. GIMSON, revised by A. CRUTTENDEN: *Gimson's Pronunciation of English* (5th edn.). Edward Arnold 1994

Chapter 5 ('Sounds in Language') is a useful supplement to our Chapter 7, and in addition provides a brief survey of the phonology of suprasegmentals.

■■□

FRANCIS KATAMBA: *An Introduction to Phonology.*
Longman 1989

In Chapter 2 Katamba introduces fundamental concepts of phonology, including the phoneme, contrast, and symmetry in phoneme inventories.

■■□

JOHN CLARK and COLIN YALLOP: *An Introduction to Phonetics and Phonology* (2nd edn.). Blackwell 1995

Chapter 4 ('The phonemic organization of speech') covers the basic theory of the phoneme and many related theoretical matters that are too complex to cover in the present book.

Chapter 8
Connected speech and coarticulation

■□□

MARTIN BALL and JOAN RAHILLY: *Phonetics: The Science of Speech.* Edward Arnold 1999

Chapter 7 covers a number of topics in this area, including consonant articulations with double (or 'secondary') constrictions, coarticulation and the representation of continuous speech by 'parametric' diagrams.

■■□

JOHN CLARK and COLIN YALLOP: *An Introduction to Phonetics and Phonology* (2nd edn.). Blackwell 1995

Clark and Yallop, on pages 82–91, explain how the facts of coarticulation and the effects of context affect our way of looking at phonemic analysis.

■■■

W. J. HARDCASTLE and N. HEWLETT (eds.): *Coarticulation: Theory, Data and Techniques.* Cambridge University Press 1999

This book contains a collection of papers which reflect current research and theory in this field.

Chapter 9
Variation

■■□

A. RADFORD, M. ATKINSON, D. BRITAIN, H. CLAHSEN and A. SPENCER: *Linguistics: An Introduction.* Cambridge University Press 1999

Chapter 3 ('Sound Variation') of this introductory textbook gives a simple overview of variation with some interesting examples.

■■□

JENNIFER JENKINS: *The Phonology of English as an International Language.* Oxford University Press 2000

An interesting and important discussion of the way English is pronounced when used as an international language, with some throught-provoking ideas about standards and teaching priorities.

■■■

JOHN WELLS: *Accents of English.* Cambridge University Press 1982

This three-volume work gives a large amount of information about the way English is pronounced around the world, and also has much to say about the analysis of variation in speech.

SECTION 4
Glossary

Page references to Section 1, Survey, are given at the end of each entry.

accent A variety of a language which is distinguished from others exclusively in terms of pronunciation: cf. **dialect**. [5, 64]. Also: A distinctive **pitch** movement in English and similar languages in which certain **syllables** are marked as distinctive or important by higher **tone**. [28, 33]

acoustics The study of the physical properties of sound. [7, 39]

affricate A **consonant** which starts as a **plosive**, but instead of ending with **plosion**, ends with a **fricative** made in the same place. [23, 45]

airstream One of several possible types of air-flow used in speech to generate sounds. [20, 24]

allophone One of the possible **realizations** of a **phoneme**. [7, 17, 49]

alveolar A **place of articulation** where the tongue touches the ridge just behind the upper front teeth. [22]

amplitude The amount of energy present in a sound wave at a particular moment in time. [40]

aperiodic Type of sound wave which does not have a regularly repeating pattern of vibration, and is typical of **fricatives**. *See also* **periodic**. [40]

approximant A class of **consonant** produced with little obstruction to the flow of air. [24, 45]

articulator Part of the **vocal tract** with which we produce speech sounds; used as a reference point for classifying **consonants**. [11, 21]

aspiration Noise produced by the rapid flow of air from the **larynx** through the **vocal tract**; usually found after the release of **plosive** consonants in some languages. [23, 44]

assimilation The process whereby a speech sound is modified so that it becomes more similar to a neighbouring sound. *See also* **coarticulation** [53]

back A kind of **vowel** in the production of which the back of the tongue is raised, e.g. [u]. [19, 42]

BBC accent The **accent** used by most English-born announcers and newsreaders on serious BBC radio and television channels; proposed as a standard accent for the description of the English spoken in England: cf. **Received Pronunciation** (**RP**). [6, 48, 63]

bilabial Term for the **place of articulation** of **consonants** produced with the upper and lower lips. [21]

cardinal vowels A set of **vowels** devised by phoneticians as a standard or reference set of vowels that do not belong to any one language. [19]

close A kind of **vowel** in which the tongue is raised close to the roof of the mouth. [18, 42]

coarticulation The overlap of the articulatory movements for different sounds, causing modifications to those sounds. *See also* **assimilation** *and* Texts 18 and 19. [53, 57]

consonant A class of speech sound which normally causes an obstruction to the flow of air and is usually found at the beginning or end of a **syllable** rather than in the middle of it. *See also* Texts 3 and 4. [5, 20, 48]

dental The **place of articulation** of **consonants** where the tongue makes contact with the upper or lower front teeth. [22]

devoicing A process that results in a sound which is normally **voiced** being pronounced as **voiceless**. [54]

dialect A variety of language which is distinguished from others in terms of vocabulary and grammar as well as pronunciation: cf. **accent**. [64]

diphthong A gliding movement from one **vowel** to another. [48]

discourse Language seen from the point of view of information structure, the interaction between language users, and the background knowledge which speakers and hearers share. [35]

downdrift The gradual lowering of **pitch** levels (usually in a **tone language**) from the beginning to the end of a stretch of speech. [28]

downstep A phenomenon found in some **tone languages**, where a high **tone** is produced on a lower **pitch** than expected when it occurs in the context of certain other tones. [28]

duration The amount of physical time for which something (for example, a speech sound) lasts. [46]

egressive Characteristic of an **airstream** which moves outwards from the body: cf. **ingressive**. [24]

elision The apparent disappearance of a speech sound where it would be expected to occur; this is usually the result of a fast speech rate. [53, 61]

filter In **acoustics**, a system which reduces or removes energy at some **frequencies** while allowing energy to pass freely at other frequencies. *See also* **source**. [41]

flap A very brief speech sound in which the tongue is curled back, then flicked forward against the **alveolar** ridge. [23, 45]

formant One of the bands or peaks of energy (the result of the **vocal tract** acting as a **filter**) which give a **vowel** or vowel-like sound its characteristic quality. [41, 42]

frequency In **acoustics**, the measure of how many times per second a pattern of vibration is repeated. *See also* **pitch**. [40]

fricative A class of **consonant** made by obstructing the flow of air enough to create a hissing noise at a particular place in the **vocal tract**. [21, 23, 43]

front A kind of **vowel** in the production of which the front of the tongue is raised, e.g. [i]; cf. **back**. [19, 42]

fundamental frequency The lowest **frequency** that can be found in a **periodic waveform**. In speech, this is almost always the frequency of vibration of the **vocal folds**. *See also* **pitch**. [46]

glottal The **place of articulation** of **consonants** produced with the **vocal folds** in the **larynx**. [22]

glottal stop A **plosive consonant** with **glottal place of articulation**. [14]

glottalic The **airstream** produced by closing the **vocal folds** and moving the **larynx** upwards (to push air out) or downwards (to pull air in). [24]

ingressive Characteristic of an **airstream** which moves into the body: cf. **egressive**. [24]

intensity A measure of the amount of energy in a sound wave; often used informally as synonymous with **amplitude**, to which it is closely related. Strictly speaking, the calculation of intensity involves the area over which the energy is distributed. [46]

International Phonetic Alphabet (IPA) A set of symbols and conventions adopted by the International Phonetic Association (ab. IPA) as a universal system for the transcription of speech sounds. [5, 8, 18]

intonation The use of **pitch** variation to convey meaning. It is normally distinguished from **tone** by the fact that tone is usually a property of individual words, while intonation patterns are more frequently properties of longer stretches of speech. It is more difficult to define the function of intonation than it is of tones. [31, 33]

isochronous A property of **rhythm** which identifies it as being composed of equal intervals of time. [37]

labiodental The **place of articulation** of **consonants** made by a constriction between the upper lip and the lower teeth. [22]

larynx Part of the **vocal tract**, containing the **vocal folds**. [13]

lateral An **approximant** sound made when the centre of the tongue is in close contact with the roof of the mouth and air escapes along the sides of the tongue. [24]

linguistic phonetics An alternative name for **phonology**; the name suggests a more phonetically oriented field of study than the rather abstract subject of phonology. [47]

manner of articulation Part of the standard way of classifying **consonants**, referring to the type of obstruction to the flow of air made by a consonant. [20, 23]

nasal Type of **consonant** in which the flow of air is prevented from escaping through the mouth, and escapes instead past the lowered **soft palate** and out through the nostrils. [13, 23, 44]

nasalization Modification of a speech sound (usually a vowel) resulting in some of the flow of air being allowed to escape through the nose. [20, 56]

neuromuscular Concerns the control of the **articulators** by the interaction of nerve fibres and muscles. [57]

open A kind of **vowel** in which the tongue is low in the mouth, e.g. [ɑ]; cf. **close**. [18]

palatal The **place of articulation** of **consonants** made by contact between the tongue and the **palate**. [22]

palate Also known as the 'hard palate' or the 'roof of the mouth'; the upper surface of the mouth where there is bone beneath the skin: cf. **soft palate**. [14]

paralinguistic feature A type of feature that forms part of **prosody**; generally considered to be outside the set of phonological contrasts of a language which can be shown to form a limited set. [37]

periodic In **acoustics**, a pattern of vibration which repeats itself at regular intervals; typical of **vowels**. [40]

pharyngeal The **place of articulation** of a **consonant** formed by constricting the **pharynx**. [22]

pharynx The tube-like passage in the throat which connects the **larynx** to the upper part of the **vocal tract**. [14]

phonation An alternative name for **voicing**, the vibration of the **vocal folds**. [13]

phoneme A speech sound which can be identified as one of the set of distinctive sounds of a particular language. [7, 10, 17]

phonemic *See* **transcription**.

phonetic *See* **transcription**.

phonology The study of the distinctive sound units of a language, the patterns they form, and the rules which regulate their use. [47]

pitch The sensation which corresponds to the **fundamental frequency** of a **periodic** sound, varying between high and low. [13, 25, 46]

pitch-accent A distinctive **pitch** level or pitch movement which makes a **syllable** seem strongly stressed. [28]

place of articulation Part of the standard way of classifying **consonants**, this refers to the place in the **vocal tract** where the flow of air is obstructed [20, 21]

plosion Short burst of noise produced by the escape of compressed air when the closure of a **plosive** consonant is released. [23]

plosive A type of **consonant** in which the flow of air is completely stopped for a short time. [20, 23, 44]

post-alveolar The **place of articulation** of **consonants** in which the tongue makes contact with the front part of the palate, just behind the **alveolar** area. [22, 24]

prosody The **suprasegmental features** of speech such as **pitch**, loudness, **tempo**, and **voice quality**. [31]

pulmonic An airstream created by the action of the lungs. [24]

realization The physical event of producing a **phoneme** as audible sound. [17]

Received Pronunciation (RP) A name given to the **accent** used as a standard for describing British English pronunciation for most of the 20th century and still in use: cf. **BBC accent**. [6, 63]

retroflex This term is traditionally said to refer to a **place of articulation** of **consonants**, but refers, in fact, to the curling backwards of the tip of the tongue, something which can happen in vowels as well as consonants. [22]

rhythm In phonetics, the occurrence of units of speech at recognizably regular intervals of time. *See also* **syllable-timed, stress-timed**. [36]

sandhi The process whereby phonological units receive different **realizations** because of the context in which they occur. *See also* **assimilation, coarticulation**. [27]

segment In phonetics, the smallest unit that can be identified in continuous speech. [5]

soft palate The flap of soft tissue which forms the continuation of the **palate** at the back of the mouth, and may be lowered to permit **nasalization** or **nasal consonants**. Another name for the soft palate is 'velum'. [14, 56]

source In speech **acoustics**, sound energy generated by an obstruction to the flow of air, such as the vibrating **vocal folds**, which is then modified by the **vocal tract** acting as a **filter**. [41]

spectral analysis The process of mathematically breaking down the complex **waveform** of speech sounds into energy at different frequencies to allow detailed analysis. [40]

spectrogram A visual display of the results of the **spectral analysis** of speech, in the form of a grey-and-white or coloured picture. [40]

stress A property of **syllables** by which they are made more noticeable or prominent than other syllables. [31, 33]

stress-timed A type of speech **rhythm** which is seen in the regularity in the intervals between stressed **syllables**. *See also* **isochronous**. [36]

suprasegmental features Features of speech (such as **pitch**) which are usually a property of stretches of speech longer than the individual segment. [31, 46]

syllable A phonological unit consisting of a **vowel** and any **consonants** which form its beginning or end. [11, 26]

syllable-timed A type of speech **rhythm** which is the result of temporal regularity in the production of all the **syllables** in an utterance. [37]

tap A very brief speech sound in which the tongue is flicked up against the roof of the mouth, interrupting the flow of air. [23, 45]

tempo The speed at which a speaker produces speech; often measured in **syllables** per second. [31, 37].

tone A distinctive **pitch** level or pitch movement found on **syllables** particularly in **tone languages**. [25]

tone language A language in which some or all of the **syllables** carry **tones** which distinguish meanings. [25]

trachea The 'wind pipe' passing up from the lungs to the **vocal tract** beginning with the **larynx**. [13]

transcription, phonemic The representation of speech in written form using only the agreed symbols for the **phonemes** of the language being transcribed. [7]

transcription, phonetic The representing of speech in written form by the use of phonetic symbols. *See also* **IPA**. [5]

trill A speech sound in which an **articulator** such as the **uvula**, tongue-tip, or lips vibrates in the **airstream**. [23, 45]

uvula The end of the **soft palate**, which hangs down above the back of the tongue near the **pharynx**. [14]

uvular A **place of articulation** where the back of the tongue touches the extreme lower end of the **soft palate**. [22]

velar A **place of articulation** where the back of the tongue touches the velum or **soft palate**. [22]

velaric An **airstream** made by sliding the tongue backwards or forwards in the mouth to move air inwards or outwards. [24]

velum *See* **soft palate**.

vocal folds Two flaps of soft tissue in the **larynx** which can be brought together or moved apart. They are used for a number of purposes in speech. *See also* **fundamental frequency, glottal, glottal stop, phonation, voice quality**. [13]

vocal tract The connected passages inside the head which form the system used to produce speech. This starts at the **larynx** and includes the **pharynx**, the mouth, and the nasal cavity. [13]

voice quality One of the **suprasegmental features** of speech that can be controlled by speakers. It is normally treated as **paralinguistic**. [31, 37]

voiced A speech sound in which the **vocal folds** are vibrating. [13, 20]

voiceless A speech sound in which the **vocal folds** are not vibrating; the vocal folds are normally moved apart to prevent vibration, though the same effect can be produced by firm closure of the vocal folds. [13, 20]

voicing The vibration of the **vocal folds** which accompanies many speech sounds, particularly vowels. [13, 20]

vowel A class of speech sound in which there is little or no obstruction to the flow of air through the **vocal tract**, and which is normally found forming the middle of a **syllable**. *See also* Texts 3 and 4. [5, 18, 42, 48]

waveform In speech acoustics, the most basic way of representing the pattern of vibration of a speech sound. [39]

Acknowledgements

The authors and publisher are grateful to those who have given permission to reproduce extracts and adaptations of copyright material:

Arnold Publishers for permission to reproduce extracts from *Gimson's Pronunciation of English*, 5th edition revised by Alan Cruttenden and from *Urban Voices* edited by Paul Foulkes and Gerard Docherty.

R. J. Baken for permission to reproduce an extract from *Clinical Measurement of Speech and Voice* by R. J. Baken.

Blackwell Publishers for permission to reproduce extracts from *An Introduction to Phonetics and Phonology* 2nd edition by John Clark and Colin Yallop, 1995; *The Handbook of Phonetic Sciences* by W. J. Hardcastle and J. Laver, 1997; and *The Dialects of England* 2nd edition by Peter Trudgill.

Cambridge University Press for permission to reproduce extracts from: *An Outline of English Phonetics* 9th edition, 1975, by D. Jones; *The Handbook of The International Phonetic Association*, 1999; *Intonation* 2nd edition, 1997, by A. Cruttenden (ed.); *English Phonology* by H. Giegerich, 1992; *From Patterns of Sound* by I. Maddieson, 1984.

Edinburgh University Press for permission to reproduce extracts from *Elements of General Phonetics* by David Abercrombie (Edinburgh University Press, 1967).

W. H. Freeman and Co./Worth Publishers for permission to reproduce an extract from *The Speech Chain* by P. Denes and E. Pinson. Copyright © Freeman 1993.

Harcourt Brace for permission to adapt excerpts from *A Course in Phonetics*, 4th edition, by Peter Ladefoged. Copyright © 2000 Harcourt Inc.

Holt, Rinehart and Winston for permission to adapt excerpts from *Phonology: Theory and Analysis* by Larry Hyman. Copyright © 1975 Holt, Rinehart and Winston.

International Phonetic Association Chart from www2.arts.gla.ac.uk/ipa/ reproduced by permission of International Phonetic Association, Prof. J. Esling, Secretary, Department of Linguistics, University of Victoria, Canada.

Mosby Inc. for permission to reproduce an extract from *Principles of Experimental Phonetics* by N. J. Lass. Mosby Year Book Inc. 1996.

Penguin Books for permission to reproduce an extract from *Phonetics* by J. D. O'Connor. Copyright © J. D. O'Connor, 1973.

University of Michigan Press for permission to reproduce an extract from *Tone Languages* by Kenneth L. Pike (Ann Arbor: The University of Michigan, 1948).

Although every effort has been made to trace and contact copyright holders before publication, this has not always been possible. We apologize for any apparent infringement of copyright and if notified, the publisher will be pleased to rectify any errors or omissions at the earliest opportunity.